The Age
of Uncertainty

John Kenneth
Galbraith

VOLUME TWO

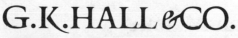
 Boston, Massachusetts

1977

Library of Congress Cataloging in Publication Data

Galbraith, John Kenneth, 1908-
    The age of uncertainty.

    Based on a BBC television series scheduled for release in 1977.
    Large print ed.
    Includes index.
    1. Economics-History. 2. Economic history.
I Title.
[HB75.G27 1977b]   330'.09   77-23077
ISBN 0-8161-6505-X

Published in Large Print by arrangement with Houghton Mifflin Company

Set in Compugraphic 18 pt English Times

A portion of this book has appeared in *Horizon*

For Adrian Malone
With admiration and gratitude

Foreword
On The Age of Uncertainty   1

VOLUME I   5
1. The Prophets and Promise
    of Classical Capitalism   9
2. The Manners and Morals
    of High Capitalism   61
3. The Dissent of Karl Marx   118
4. The Colonial Idea   183
5. Lenin and the Great Ungluing   226
6. The Rise and Fall of Money   281

VOLUME II
7. The Mandarin Revolution   339
8. The Fatal Competition   396
9. The Big Corporation   451
10. Land and People   499
11. The Metropolis   537
12. Democracy, Leadership,
    Commitment   577

    A Major Word of Thanks   619
    Notes   625

    Index   635

6.
The Rise and Fall of Money

Money is a singular thing.* It ranks with love as man's greatest source of joy. And it ranks with death as his greatest source of anxiety. Over all history it has oppressed nearly all people in one of two ways: either it has been abundant and very

*In 1973, when the BBC series on *The Age of Uncertainty* was being planned, I prepared a memorandum on the subject of money for the guidance of my colleagues in the enterprise. In the process of amplification and revision it became a rather lengthy book and was published as such in 1975. (*Money: Whence It Came, Where It Went.* Boston: Houghton Mifflin, and London: André Deutsch.) There are echoes of the book in the pages following. Anyone who has read it can, with the very best conscience, omit this chapter and, though less conscientiously, the next.

unreliable, or reliable and very scarce. However, for many there has been a third affliction: for them money has been both unreliable and scarce.

For studying the full range of human emotion, the next best thing to the psychiatrist's couch is, perhaps, the modern supermarket. It could be why the modern politician goes there to solicit votes. People entering or emerging from a supermarket are in the grip of their most common fears, are deeply sensitive, accordingly, to the political issues that bear upon this anxiety. In times of depression or recession they are wondering if their money will continue, if they will have any to spend the next time they push a cart. In times of boom and inflation they are asking themselves if next time there will be anything to buy that they can still afford.

In recent years this last worry has been the worst. It is the special terror of the person whose days of work are over, whose income for the rest of life is given and will never, by any magic, increase. What if that money ceases to buy enough to sustain life or, what may be equally important, to maintain accustomed respectability? But there is equally the anxiety of the person who does not know whether next week's purchases will be supported by a job. Is a layoff in prospect? How long will the unemployment last? How will I, or we, get by?

The anxiety in the supermarket has its focus on money. It is one of the great uncertainties of life. It has been so for a long time. More than most things, an understanding of money requires an appreciation of its history. What was once simple has become complex. But if we see how money has evolved — if we take the complexities one by one as they were added by its history — an understanding of the final result is not so difficult. We see with fair ease the uncertainties of which it is the focus.

The Origins

Money has been an everyday fact of life for at least 2500 years. Herodotus, more or less as an afterthought and with a nice juxtaposition of concepts, tells of the invention of coined money in Asia Minor:

> All of the young women of Lydia prostitute themselves, by which they procure their marriage portion . . . The manners and customs of the Lydians do not essentially vary from those of Greece, except in this prostitution of the young women. They are the first people on record who coined gold and silver into money, and traded in retail.[1]

It seems certain that there were much earlier experiences with coinage in the Indus Valley and China of which Herodotus was unaware.

For the next many centuries, a few brief episodes apart, no one receiving coined money could be quite sure what he or she was getting; few inventions ever lent themselves more profitably to abuse. The coin might be of its proclaimed weight of gold and silver. It might be less. It might have a lesser metal melted in. Banks and governments made promises to pay such coin as a substitute for money, and the promises then became money. Abuse of these promises was one of the few inventions more profitable than mistreating coins. The measure of the abuse was the grave uncertainty on the part of the recipient as to what he was getting and the counterpart uncertainty as to what that money would buy.

Then, in the last century, money became reliable. The major problems of its mismanagement seemed solved. What now became uncertain was the opportunity for earning it; jobs, farm prices, the earnings of the small businessman were anything but secure.

It was World War I that showed that the new reliability of money was an illusion. Along with the old political systems monetary stability also came unglued. There would be greater uncertainty than ever about getting money. And there would again be uncertainty as to what it would buy.

Most of us, whether we admit it or not, live with a linear view of history. We think that, over a long enough span of time, men learn, things improve. The history of money gives no support for this optimism.

The Function

Though one begins the history of money with the invention of coinage — the stamping or minting of pieces of metal of a specific (claimed) weight and quality — this is quite arbitrary. Cattle, shells, chunks of metal, whiskey, tobacco have also been used. They perform the essential function of money, which is to avoid the awkwardness of barter — the natural difficulty of finding someone who wishes to trade cattle or whiskey directly for a house. What serves as money need only be durable, reasonably uniform and evident as to quality. It can then be held for a time and will be generally acceptable to buyers and sellers. Given these qualities, almost anything will serve as an intermediate stage in transactions. In nonpastoral societies it is also helpful if it can be carried or kept around the house. Coins came into use because they were durable, improved on chunks or sacks of gold and silver by being in predetermined amounts, and could be carried in a purse. Scales for weighing the metal were no longer needed, at least in the comparatively rare instances where the weight of the coins could be trusted.

Coins, although not many have noticed it, are now obsolescent. They no longer figure in major transactions. They survive only as minor change, for occasional nervous hoarding, as collectors' items and as an adjunct to slot machines. They are only an attenuated reminder, a souvenir, of what was once all money.

Banks and Money

After coins came banks. They flourished in Roman times, reached a high level of development in Venice, Florence and Genoa. With banks came the power, given to few private citizens, to create money.

It may be why bankers are so solemn. A certain responsibility is involved. For a full view of banks and money the city to visit is Amsterdam. It is associated with not one but two of the great developments in their history.

In 1609, money — hard, coined money — was, as money goes, abundant in Amsterdam. Mostly it was silver, an important point. Through most of history silver, not gold, was the primary metal for coinage. That Judas got silver for Jesus does not mean there was anything derogatory about the payment, only that it was, for the time, a normal commercial transaction. Following the voyages of Columbus, silver mines of unparalleled richness had been discovered in the New World, principally in Mexico. In the sixteenth century this metal flooded into Europe to demonstrate one of the fundamental propositions regarding money: the more abundant the money, *everything else equal,* the less it will buy. As silver became abundant, prices are believed to have risen almost everywhere in Europe. A good many people who hadn't heard about the discovery of America saw its effects in the price of whatever trifle they had to buy.

Though silver and silver coins were abundant, another firm proposition concerning money was also demonstrated in these years. However much they have, people feel they can do with more of it. So everywhere in Europe men were taking the coins and sweating and clipping them, thereby getting metal to make more of them. In 1606, the Dutch Parliament had issued a manual for money changers. It listed 846 silver and gold coins, many of them appallingly deficient in weight and purity. Such was the state of abuse that no one, when he sold goods for money, could be sure what he was getting. It was to this problem of quality that the merchants of Amsterdam now addressed themselves. They created a bank owned by the city; the bank solved the problem of the quality of the coins by going back to the system that antedated the invention of coinage. That was weighing.

In this action the town fathers pioneered the idea of public regulation of the money supply by a public bank. A merchant brought his good and wretched coins to the bank, the bank weighed them, and the weight of the pure metal was then credited to his account. This deposit was a highly reliable form of money. A merchant could transfer it to the account of another merchant. The recipient knew that he was getting honest weight, nothing funny. Payments through the bank commanded a premium.

Then came the second Amsterdam discovery, although the principle was known elsewhere. The deposits so created did not need to be left idly in the bank. They could be lent. The bank then got interest. The borrower then had a deposit that *he* could spend. But the original deposit still stood to the credit of the original depositor. That too could be spent. Money, spendable money, had been created. Let no one rub his or her eyes. It's still being done — every day. The creation of money by a bank is as simple as this, so simple, I've often said, that the mind is slightly repelled.

The important thing, obviously, is that

the original depositor and the borrower must never come at the same time for their deposits — their money. They must trust their bank. They must trust it to the extent of believing it isn't doing what it does as a matter of course. That is the thin edge on which creation of money by a bank always rests.

The Amsterdam Scene

In the first hundred years after the founding of the bank, the city of Amsterdam grew wonderfully; the population and area greatly expanded. The arts — painting and music — flourished. After 1631, the city had a fair claim to being considered the center of the whole art world, for it was in that year that Rembrandt moved there from Leyden. The Merchant City, as we shall later see, was a place of great good taste. Amsterdam, the most eminent merchant city of its age, is very good evidence for the case. Many houses from this time survive. Some are still in the possession of the same families. One, that of the merchant Jan Six, is as lovely as any in Europe. Among the forty-odd paintings by Dutch masters still in the possession of the family are no fewer than three by Rembrandt. Rembrandt was a friend, and his name is prominent in the guest book of the time.

It is tempting to attribute the prosperity of Amsterdam and the consequent flowering of the artistic spirit to the excellence and stability of its financial institutions and particularly to the Bank of Amsterdam. Bankers would applaud; David Rockefeller would be especially pleased. There were other factors.

Amsterdam was admirably situated on what, with some canal-digging, became one of the outlets of the Rhine. It was, like all successful merchant cities, a tolerant place; men who wanted to make money could do business here regardless of race, creed or national origin. Much of Amsterdam's prosperity was the achievement of its large settlement of Huguenots and Portuguese and Spanish Jews. The city had a reputation for doing business with anyone who wished to do business, including, on occasion, those who might be fighting the Dutch. But, unquestionably, the Bank helped.

I should complete its story. As will now be evident, every monetary innovation or reform carries the seeds of some new abuse. So it was here. One of the important borrowers from the Bank was the Dutch East India Company. The members of the Company were often the same men who ran the Bank. With the passage of time, lending and borrowing became incestuous, even narcissistic. Nothing is new; the failure of the Franklin National Bank in New York in the nineteen-seventies, the London and County in the same years in England, was partly the result of bankers lending to business firms which they greatly admired and trusted because they were their own. In the eighteenth century the East India Company fell on hard times; there was war with England, ships did not come back. It was slow to pay at first, and then its loans went into default. The making of loans and the creation of money by a bank, to repeat, is only possible if depositors do not come all at once for their money. If they suspect that they can't get their money, they will surely come. Suspected weakness ensures weakness.

Early in the last century suspicion spread, the weakness was affirmed. The depositors started coming, and they couldn't be paid. In 1819, after two centuries of service, the Bank of Amsterdam was wound up. By then, however, there had been a far more spectacular demonstration of how a bank can create money and how this ability can be abused.

Paris, 1719

Louis XIV died in 1715. His legacy to France was great and varied, and it included two major misfortunes. One was the French Treasury which was bankrupt; the other was the Regent, the Duc d'Orléans, who was intellectually and morally bankrupt. The result was the seemingly hopeless situation that gives opportunity to a rascal, someone who promises by magic or legerdemain to put everything right. Men who are desperate for a solution are easy to persuade because they wish desperately to be persuaded. The Duc d'Orléans was an especially easy case.

The available rascal we have already encountered. He was John Law, and to this day some historians regret the word rascal. Perhaps he was a genius who got carried away by his own achievements.

He had a background in financial matters. His father was a well-to-do Edinburgh goldsmith. In that time goldsmiths, since they had to have good strongboxes, stored valuables and coins for other people, and by this service had become bankers. On the Continent Law was engaged in selling an idea for a new kind of bank, the deposits of which would be secured by land rather than by silver or gold. He was also avoiding English justice; he had been unduly successful in a duel.

In Paris in 1716, he got permission from the Regent to establish a bank, the Banque Royale. As part of the bargain the bank took over the debts of the Regent and of the realm. These debts were then paid off with notes of the bank, promises by the bank to pay off the face value to the holders in silver or gold. It is not hard to see how the Regent was persuaded.

Then in 1717, Law organized the Company of the West, later the Company of the Indies but known ever afterward as the Mississippi Company. There was no doubt as to its assets; potentially they were greater than those of any company before or since. It held absolute title to all land north from the Gulf of Mexico to Minnesota and east from the Rockies to the Alleghenies.

This spacious endowment served Law's purposes in two ways. The notes that his bank was issuing were backed, as noted, by gold and silver. The needs of the Regent being large, so was the issue of notes. By no stretch of the imagination was there enough gold and silver in France to redeem the notes, so the imagination of the note-holders was stretched to include Louisiana. There, it was said, gold and silver were in unlimited supply. As I've told in an earlier chapter, maps of the period showed the mines, although no one has seen them since. The nonexistent metal in the imaginary mines was the backing for the notes.

But Parisians were by now in a trusting mood. Hearing of these conceptual riches and that colonization was under way to get them, they rushed to buy the stock of the Company of the West. The stock boomed. Law helped the price along by sundry forms of thimblerigging and fiduciary levitation. In a strong market some well-timed purchases of stock, in combination with some suitably reckless promises, will send up prices and attract the buyers who will send them up much more. By 1719, the boom had become a wild speculation. The price of the stock went up, sometimes by the hour. The old Paris Bourse was outdoors in the Rue Quincampoix. The excitement was intense and even violent, and the noise was hideous. Crowds swarmed also to the Place Vendôme, to Law's headquarters. Some hoped only to catch a glimpse of him; some, on one pretext or another, tried to get inside. Those who got inside asked Law to sell them stock. Women investors, the histories tell, offered themselves as an added inducement. This must have been an unprecedented experience for someone from Scotland.

The year 1719 in Paris was truly a wonderful time. Law's notes went out by the hundreds of millions. Government creditors who were paid off in the notes then rushed to buy stock in the Banque Royale or in the Mississippi Company. From the money so invested more could be lent to the government, yet more notes could go out and yet more stock could be sold. It was a complete closed-circle system for recycling worthless paper. In consequence, all involved were getting rich — on or in paper. It is to that year that we owe the useful French word "millionaire."

In 1719, John Law was the most famous man in all France. He was ennobled as the Duc d'Arkansas, a title not revived in later years even by Congressman Wilbur Mills. On January 5, 1720, he was made Comptroller General of France, the supreme arbiter of all French finances.

There was no way to go but down, and presently this became evident. Doubts began to develop about the notes. So people started bringing them to the Banque Royale for the silver and gold that were still in Louisiana, and also not there. The Prince de Conti sent three wagons to carry back the gold to which his notes entitled him. Paying off the notes in gold and silver was suspended; in modern terms, the Banque Royale went off the gold (and silver) standard. And, in a further, rather severe step, ownership of precious metals except in small quantities was made a crime. But nothing could disguise the elementary fact that the Banque Royale could not pay, that the notes were now worthless. Law only narrowly escaped from Paris with his life. Parisians got what pleasure they could from a song that recommended that the paper be put to the most vulgar possible use.

Law's colonization and gold mining had not been attractive to the average Parisian. Press gangs, accordingly, had been sent out to round up sundry vagabonds and even reputable citizens who were not sufficiently aware of their opportunities abroad. There was a special need for wives and a special effort to recruit what were then called women of medium virtue. Paris, in my youth, was considered a place of imaginative wickedness, a reputation long ago lost to Amsterdam, Copenhagen and Times Square. But there are still links with the past. The Rue Quincampoix is today a minor resort of women of medium virtue.

Though the end was unhappy, something was accomplished. Like the deposits in Amsterdam, Law's notes were money created by a bank. This money got the Regent out of a tight spot, encouraged colonization and made France prosperous, at least for a while. Law — a somewhat neglected point — had directed a substantial amount into canal building and other useful public works. Issued in excess, the notes clearly were a disaster. Used in moderation, might they not do good? That, now, the British were to prove.

The Bank of England

Some of the most interesting observations on John Law we owe to the Duc de Saint-Simon, the relentless chronicler of life at Versailles and in Paris during the reign of Louis XIV and after. He thought Law's bank was a good idea for any country but France. The French, he said, lacked restraint.

There is much to his case. Twenty years earlier, a fellow countryman of Law's, one William Paterson — on money, as on political economy, the early pre-eminence of the Scotch is unchallenged — had sold essentially the same idea as the Banque Royale to William of Orange. William too needed money; his debts came not from succeeding Louis but from fighting him. In 1694, the Bank of England was formed; its founders subscribed the money the King needed. In return, they were given the right to make loans to others with newly issued notes backed by the King's promise to pay. Paterson soon left, most likely, it now seems, over a conflict of interest. He was promoting a rival bank.

A few years later Scotchmen were seized with the notion that vast fortunes could be made by founding a colony (Darien) near what is now the Isthmus of Panama. It was thought, rightly, to be a strategic location. Few survived the climate and the fever. Paterson was the leading promoter of the Darien adventure. He lost his wife and children there and barely escaped with his own life.

But Paterson's bank survived and flourished, and no financial institution before or since has had such prestige. To be a member of its Court of Directors still suggests grave financial wisdom and ominous economic power. The power can be questioned. Outside directors are not told of important decisions until after they are taken. This ensures against conflict of interest, a matter on which the Bank is still vigilant. It does reduce appreciably a man's impact on the decision.

The glow extends across the seas, continues down through the generations. In the United States in past years, the Federal Reserve Board has regularly been used by American presidents as a place of deposit for men who could not reliably be trusted to balance their own checkbooks. Once in office, they are addressed with reverence as Governor and dispense deeply ambiguous judgments on the economic and financial prospect, which susceptible journalists, bankers and economists treat with the utmost respect. However illiterate, economically or otherwise, they are sustained by the reputation of the Bank of England.

In the early years of the eighteenth century the Bank was saved from a principal role in the South Sea Bubble because the South Sea Company outbid it in recklessness. Later it was thought far too generous in its loans to Pitt for the wars against Napoleon. David Ricardo held this view, although neither Ricardo nor his fellow critics offered any better ideas about where to raise the money. But, in time, the Bank became an accomplished instrument for regulating the creation of money by lesser banks — in placing limits on lending and consequent deposit expansion and note issue. In doing so, it provided the restraint that, in its absence, had brought misfortune in Amsterdam, disaster in Paris.

As the creation of money — deposits and bank notes — by banks is a simple thing, so is the mechanism for its control. In London in the eighteenth century the goldsmiths, now become the banks, made loans in notes against their holdings of gold and silver coin. The Bank of England, when it received these notes, returned them for collection in gold or silver. This required the banks to maintain reasonable reserves of cash against their note issues. They could not be reckless in the issue of notes as was Law. Later the Bank acquired for itself a monopoly of note issue, first in London, then throughout the country. It had then only to discipline itself.

The subordinate or commercial banks could still lend the funds of their depositors. This would mean deposits — money — for those who borrowed. And this money-creation could be carried to excess. The Bank of England developed a method for preventing this. When the ordinary or commercial banks seemed too generous with their loans, the Bank allowed some of its own loans to run out or it sold some of the securities it held. In repaying these loans or paying for their securities, customers of the commercial banks would transfer gold and silver from the vaults of the ordinary banks to the Bank of England. The reserves in gold and silver of the commercial banks, their protection in case depositors came for their money, would thus be depleted. Their lending and associated deposit- and money-creation would then have to be curtailed. This is the procedure now celebrated as open market operations. Another simple thing. The clearing banks, as the commercial banks are called in Britain, could replace their depleted reserves by borrowing from the Bank of England. But that could be restrained by raising the rate of interest. This charge by the Bank of England came to be called the Bank Rate, in the last century a mysterious and wonderful thing. In the United States the Bank Rate is the rediscount rate or, latterly, the discount rate.

Such were the regulatory functions as developed by the Bank of England. It found for itself one other major purpose. Recurrently there were the moments of fear and suspicion when depositors came to the clearing banks for their money, for the cash that by the nature of banking was not sufficiently there. The Bank of England would then come to the rescue and lend to the clearing banks, though at a rather stiff rate. The central bank, as banks for other bankers came to be called, served these other banks as the lender of last resort.

It wasn't always easy to rise above the panic that sent people to the clearing banks for their money and these in turn to the Bank of England. Pessimism had a way of infecting everyone, including the great men at the Bank. But it was even harder for them to fall below euphoria when, as recurrently happened, that swept the City and England. In 1720, there was a vast outbreak of company promotions with much speculation in their shares. Trade with Spanish America was the focus of excitement but there was also a notable company "for carrying on an undertaking of great advantage, but nobody to know what it is."[2] All these promotions were the South Sea Bubble, and, as noted, the Bank of England narrowly escaped involvement. A century later, in 1824, there was another wave of speculative enthusiasm, again over investment prospects in South America. Again, there was diversification. Englishmen could invest in a company "to drain the Red Sea with a view to recovering the treasure abandoned by the Egyptians after the crossing of the Jews."[3] Again the Bank was captured by the spirit of the times and did not curb the more insane lending by the banks. It's the old question: who regulates the regulators? Who is king in the world of the blind when there isn't even a one-eyed man? The problem will recur.

Still, in the last century the Bank of England showed a remarkable capacity for economic innovation. All of the functions of a modern central bank were identified and developed. Not surprisingly, then, its operations were viewed with admiration, even as high art. Victorians heard with grave attention that the Bank Rate had been raised. They did not know what it meant. But they knew that it was an act of extreme wisdom.

Paper Money

Coinage was the invention of the Greeks. The Italians, Dutch, French and English, including always the Scotch, were the developers of banks and central banking. We come now to paper money. This, in singular measure, was the gift of Americans and Canadians to the Western world.

The American colonies, all know, were greatly opposed to taxation without representation. They were also, a less celebrated quality, equally opposed to taxation with representation. It was out of this opposition to taxation that government paper money was born. The birthplace was Massachusetts; the year was 1690. Massachusetts soldiers had just returned from an unsuccessful expedition against Quebec. The loot from the fortress was to have been their pay but there was a miscalculation; Quebec did not fall. Angry soldiers can be a source of unease. So, in the absence of real money — gold or silver — they were given promises of such money instead. These promissory notes then passed from hand to hand as money.

It seemed a most painless way to pay bills. The other colonies followed suit; some, notably Rhode Island and South Carolina, issued notes in huge volume. Any thought of eventual redemption was a mirage. But the restraint that the Duc de Saint-Simon thought lacking in the French was not entirely absent in America. In the Middle Colonies — Pennsylvania, Maryland, New York — in the century before the Revolution, paper money was issued and used with good sense. It was kept reasonably scarce, its redemption in gold or silver continued to seem plausible and thus it was kept acceptable. In the view of modern historians, it was not only convenient for trade but saved these colonists from falling prices with the consequent adverse effect on business.

The prime exponent of paper money in

these years was Benjamin Franklin. He thought it a good and useful thing, and his advocacy had an intensely practical touch. He printed money for the colonial governments on his own printing press.

In London this colonial invention of paper money seemed, in contrast, a most foolish contrivance. So, toward the middle of the eighteenth century, Parliament forbade further issues of it in peacetime. Franklin journeyed to London to oppose the prohibition but was unsuccessful. The action caused much resentment in the colonies, almost as much as the taxes. This grievance has never had much standing in American history. The sound men of the colonies thought that Parliament was absolutely right. So, for a long time, did the reputable historians.

The Canadian Variant

In all countries of the world — Communist, capitalist and those which only dream of such distinction — the convention as regards paper money is now the same. It requires a rectangular slip of paper covered with suitable swirls of ink and featuring a dead hero, a Rubens figure, a cornucopia of vegetables or an heroic monument. This is partly an accident. In the development of paper money, governments followed the dull puritanical model of Massachusetts, not the irreverent and sparkling example of New France.

The Quebec model was the playing card. The French, as all know, were casual about their North American colonies. Ships and money often failed to arrive. When this happened and in roughly the same years as the Massachusetts attack, the intendants at Quebec also paid the garrison and for their supplies with promises. The most readily available and durable paper stock was playing cards. These became the promises by virtue of having the official government signature attached. Then when the ships came in, the cards were redeemed in gold or silver. The innovation shocked Versailles but, eventually, there being no better alternative, it was accepted. In a 1711 issue, spades and clubs were the currency of highest denomination; hearts and diamonds had only half their value.

As with all currencies, if too many cards were dealt, inflation resulted. In the last days of New France this happened. The pressure of need was great, the means for redemption small. At the end, the purchasing power of the cards was greatly diminished.

All must weep that, after Wolfe met Montcalm on the Plains of Abraham, this currency came to an end. Its survival would everywhere have lightened and informed financial life. At Las Vegas men and women would now play for and with the same currency. Anyone making a killing on the stock market would be rewarded in clubs and spades. A reference to gambling in Wall Street would not be a metaphor. The innocent, looking at the money they would get, would be duly warned. Had the playing cards survived, the balance sheet of the Chase Manhattan Bank would set out assets and liabilities in hearts and diamonds as well as clubs and spades. The bank's recent venture into the world of real estate trusts would have been recognized immediately for the gamble it really was.

Paper and Revolution

If one is planning a revolution, he should first, no doubt, get a cause and an army. Then, based on all experience, he — or she — should get a printing press. Revolutionary governments cannot easily levy taxes, especially if the revolt is against bad taxes. Their credit is not likely to be good so they cannot borrow. There remains only the printing of money.

Money so printed paid for the Russian Revolution. Likewise for the revolt of the Confederate States. Likewise for the French Revolution — the famous assignats were issued against the security of the church land and that of the nobility. And paper money, the invention of the colonies, paid for the American Revolution.

Some was issued by the states. The rest, the Continental notes, were authorized by the Continental Congress. A half billion dollars worth altogether was put in circulation. The predictable result, as at

Quebec, was inflation: by the end of the war a pair of shoes cost about five thousand dollars in Virginia, a full outfit around a million. But there was no alternative. Taxes could not have paid for the war. Even had the erstwhile colonists been willing, collection would have been difficult. No one thought the new republic even a passable credit risk. Paper money saved the day.

This too has never been recognized. When the war was won, the sound-money men wrote the history. They could not have it said that the United States was conceived in financial sin. So they held that the financing of the Revolution was a terrible mistake, without ever explaining what would have been both practical and right. Their view persists. The Continental note has come down to us only as a symbol of opprobrium. "Not worth a Continental!" If properly treated, it would have a place beside the Liberty Bell. The historians even edited Benjamin Franklin. His position on paper money is rarely mentioned. Children are told only that he was a good man in diplomacy, thrift and electricity.

Banks and the Central Banks

Though paper money financed the Revolution, the resulting inflation bred remorse; this has been, through history, a highly reliable result of runaway prices. There were vows that it would not happen again. In consequence, the Constitution of the United States prohibited the states from issuing paper money, even as the Westminster Parliament had done. It also, more remarkably, forbade the Federal Government to do so too. Only by a very strained interpretation of the Constitution, and after paper money — the Greenbacks — had been issued in volume during the Civil War, was such money made legal in the United States.

Banks had also been prohibited in the colonies by the British. With independence these were now legal, and, as we have sufficiently seen, they too manufactured money. And while the issue of paper money by a government had to await action by a legislature, the issue of money by a bank did not. Almost anyone could do it on very short notice and even smaller capital, and the results were wonderful. The proprietor could print notes and make loans in these notes to his friends, neighbors or himself. The notes, with luck, would be accepted in payment for horses, cattle, machinery, an anvil and forge or the initial small stock of a grocery or hardware store. The borrower would then be in business. Perhaps, with more luck, he would be able to pay off his loan. A wonderful thing, a bank. The citizens of the new republic discovered banking as an adolescent discovers sex.

There were objections, however, from the people who got the notes — from the Eastern merchants to whom they came for payment of accounts, from the more conservative Eastern bankers to whom they came for deposit. When the notes were returned for collection of the gold or silver they promised, the issuing banks were often indifferent and frequently not to be found. The Easterners wanted money that could be sent to England to buy goods and that did not lose its value from one day to the next. The obvious solution was to have a central bank on the model of the Bank of England to keep these new banks in line. No one doubted the pre-eminence of the British in financial matters. George Washington might have fought the Redcoats. But he left Barings, the great London bank, in charge of his personal finances throughout the war, and Barings did not let him down.

The Bank of England, we have seen, disciplined its subordinate banks by presenting their notes systematically for collection in silver or gold. Thus it required them to keep their loans and resulting deposits in some reasonably safe relationship to their hard cash. This would be the basic function of an American central bank. It could impose discipline and restraint on the local banks by similarly presenting their notes for collection. It was a function that the banks on the frontier thought less than necessary. They would have to make good on their bad money. And their purpose, however it might be denied, was to issue bad money for whatever it might buy.

Here were the seeds of the most persistent political conflict in American history and, after slavery, the most bitter. It was between the men who wanted good money and those who wanted the bad money that put them in business. It began with Alexander Hamilton when he redeemed the Continental notes at the distinctly extravagant rate of one cent on the dollar, the act of a sound-money man. It was continued when the First Bank of the United States was established in accordance with Hamilton's recommendations and incurred so much displeasure for its discipline that its charter in 1810 was allowed to lapse. The struggle did not end until the defeat of William Jennings Bryan in the presidential election of 1896, and there were many echoes as late as the administration of Franklin D. Roosevelt. Its high point was in the eighteen-thirties — the titanic struggle between Andrew Jackson, President of the United States, and Nicholas Biddle, President of the Second Bank of the United States.

Jackson versus Biddle

The President of the United States, Andrew Jackson, was from the frontier — Tennessee. His rough appearance and manner are part of the legend and were, for a long time, a damaging model for politicians from the West. Nicholas Biddle, polished, well-dressed, well-bathed, slightly bejeweled, was pre-eminently a member of the Establishment, as the Biddles of Philadelphia have been ever since. Writing home to his mother of his American travels, the eventual Edward VII told, after his visit to Philadelphia, of a most distinguished family called Scrapple, a most appetizing breakfast dish called biddle.

Biddle lacked the tact that the rich and successful have since developed greatly and which has perhaps become second nature. On public occasions he compared his power as President of the Second Bank of the United States with that of the President of the United States. When asked by a Senate committee if he had ever abused his financial power, he praised his own restraint. Although very few of the small banks "might not have been destroyed" by his discipline, "none has ever been injured."[4] This allowed Jackson to thunder back: "The President of the Bank has told us that most of the State banks exist by its forbearance."[5]

The historic showdown came in 1832. Early that year the friends of the Bank in Congress led by Henry Clay — Clay was also from the frontier but the forces of civilization had worked their way — renewed the charter of the Bank. Jackson responded with a stinging veto. The presidential election was then fought on the issue. Biddle had the money, and he had been generous with loans to congressmen, senators and the press. (One of the journalists in his pay was James Gordon Bennett, whose son we encountered in Newport and on the Riviera.) Andrew Jackson had the votes. He won, and the Second Bank of the United States was defeated. Biddle then got it a Pennsylvania charter but power is often a onetime thing. Very soon he went broke. The smaller local banks were to remain free from serious restraint in many of the states for a century.

Once Biddle's hand had been lifted, these state banks exploded in number. To have a bank in the eighteen-thirties became, almost literally, a human right. Many were well managed. But for many the more remote the crossroads, the deeper the forest, the more desolate the swamp, the more attractive the location. For a remote or obscure address diminished the likelihood that the notes issued by the bank would ever find their way back for collection. There was state regulation but it was far from reliable. In Michigan, where the history is better than elsewhere, the banks were required to maintain a minimum reserve of gold and silver against their notes. Boxes of coins were sent around through the forest just in front of the commissioners who were sent out to enforce the law. As an act of economy, a thin layer of gold was once found to be covering a thick deposit of broken glass. In conservative Massachusetts in these years a bank failed. Against notes of $500,000 outstanding, it had cash reserves of $86.48. By the time of the Civil War some 7000 different kinds of bank notes were in circulation in the United States; to these, numerous artists with access to a printing press had added another 5000 that were counterfeit. Legal or bogus, the purchasing power was often about the same, meaning nil.

It was too confusing, and in 1865, a few weeks before Appomattox, the right of the small banks — those chartered by the states — to issue notes was finally abolished. But by then bank deposits and bank checks were taking the place of hand-to-hand money. Nothing prevented the banks from creating money by making loans and creating deposits. This they continued to do. Often it was in the same open-handed way that they had made the loans that were taken away in bank notes.

Gold

The United States in the last century was, or seemed on money to be, a maverick case. While wildcat banking flourished, especially on the American frontier, the major countries of Europe were accepting the lessons of Britain and the Bank of England on how banking should be regulated. They were also resolving, it seemed for all time, the question of the kind of metal into which bank notes, bank deposits and government notes would be converted. Silver and gold had for centuries been in competition. It was confusing to have two metals; they changed in value in relation to each other, and the one that was cheaper always got passed on. The one of more value people held. In 1867, the leading nations of Europe met in Paris and resolved that, henceforth, their business would all be done in gold.

The course of events in the United States was different. The Civil War, like the Revolutionary War, had been financed (though much less extensively) by paper money. When prices fell after the war, there were powerful demands, particularly from the farmers, that the Greenbacks be retained. And when great deposits of silver were later discovered in the West, the miners joined with the farmers in a crusade to keep silver. William Jennings Bryan, in memorable oratory, invoked Jesus and the Crucifixion against gold.

But eventually even the United States conformed. By the turn of the century the Greenbackers belonged to history. Bryan had been defeated on the issue of free coinage of silver. Then in the United States, as in Europe, gold became the only metal into which other money, if good, could be converted, and this convertibility was now general. In Western countries the gold standard, as such convertibility is called, was almost everywhere the rule.

Although the impression is now to the contrary, the gold standard was in effect only for a few years. World War I swept the gold out of Europe to buy munitions. This destroyed the gold standard there. It brought gold to the United States in such plenitude that it was far too abundant to serve as money here. The gold standard never functioned effectively again. It too was a prime casualty of the great ungluing.

Uncertainty: Old and New

A world in which all money could be exchanged into gold coins or their equivalent has always seemed marvelously certain. Whatever its defects, there was, indeed, a high certainty about what such money could buy. Over the whole of the last century prices fell, the purchasing power of gold or gold-based money increased.

This certainty, a sadly neglected point, was always greatest for those with money. When the Bank of England raised the Bank Rate or moved otherwise to restrain the banks and ensure that they would have the gold to meet the demands of their depositors, business firms were denied loans. In further consequence, prices fell and jobs were lost. For the farmers and workers so affected, the gold standard was a source of insecurity. The purchasing power of the money was maintained; it was only that they now had less or none. The difference was that, unlike the rich, these citizens were inarticulate and usually innocent of the causes of their misfortune.

(On this matter American farmers were much less innocent than most.) Latter-day admirers of the gold standard, and of stern monetary management in general, have but rarely understood that its success in the last century owed much to the helplessness of those who were subject to its discipline. As economic life expanded in Britain and elsewhere in Europe, so did the number of workers who were subject to the uncertainty of employment and income that went with sound central-banking practice. So did the unwillingness to accept it. To the consequences of this I will return.

The United States, we have seen, rejected central banks and opted instead for giving the local banker the right to create the bank notes and the bank deposits that put the local farmers and merchants in business. This too had its uncertainties, and these too were severe. Banks would be created; the loans of the new banks and the old would finance a euphoric speculation in land, canals, railroads, commodities or industrial shares. Then would come the crash, and the banks would fail by the score. This cycle continued on into the present century with increasing severity. From crash to crash was usually around twenty years — just time for the memory of the last disaster to fade. Each boom was duly heralded as the response to a new era; doubters were invariably dismissed as men incapable of appreciating the opportunities for gain by which those of true vision were being enriched. After each crash politicians called for confidence. Things were much better than they seemed. Men of financial wisdom counseled patience and, on occasion, prayer. In the panic of 1907, J. P. Morgan took an even more forthright step. He called together the Protestant clergymen of New York City and adjured them to tell their congregations the next Sunday to leave their money in the banks. It was a time for affirming faith, and that included faith in the banking system.

Despite such calming counsel, when panic struck, prices fell, men lost their jobs and banks failed. The bank failures added greatly to the severity of the crash.

For then deposits in failed banks were no longer usable money; people no longer had it to spend. This had an astringent effect on business. And the surviving banks, now suffering badly from fright, ceased making the loans that created money. The monetary system was thus superbly arranged to cancel or reduce the money supply precisely when this would do the most to make things worse.

The culminating crash came in 1929. In the next four years around nine thousand banks bit the dust, a third of all the banks in the country. With each failure individuals and companies lost money they would otherwise have spent, loans they would otherwise have received. And the surviving banks battened down against the day when their depositors would come. Then, on March 6, 1933, all the banks in the United States were closed. Except for what little was in hand, the money came to a full stop. Ten years before, Germany had been buried in an avalanche of reichsmarks in an inflation that is not forgotten to this day. Finally it stabilized at a thousand billion of the old currency to one of the new. Now the United States, for practical purposes, had no money. It cannot be doubted that, after 2500 years, there was still much to be learned about the management of money.

The Federal Reserve System

This was a saddening discovery. In 1914, the gold standard had seemed forever. So also in that year it seemed that the uncertainties of the American banking system, those that produced the continuing cycles of boom and bust, had finally been corrected. On almost exactly the day that the guns of August began to sound, the victory of Andrew Jackson over the Eastern financial establishment was finally reversed. The United States set up a central bank. More exactly, in a compromise designed to overcome the old hostility, it established twelve central banks and a co-ordinating body of ill-defined power in Washington. This was the Federal Reserve System.

The Federal Reserve System has always been greatly loved by economists; it even has a nasty but affectionate nickname, The Fed. There was little to be loved in its early performance. No one knew for sure who was in charge — Washington, the regional Banks in Kansas City, St. Louis, San Francisco. Or was it the New York Bank with its special advantage of being in the financial capital?

More serious was an instinct, one that was evident in the earliest days of the Bank of England, for whatever action made things worse. In the years following World War I, there was sharp speculation in farm commodities and farm real estate — the boom of 1919 - 20. The Federal Reserve Banks looked on tolerantly while banks made the loans that financed this boom. Then came the crash of 1920 - 21. Now the Federal Reserve clamped down on bank lending and helped to make the resulting depression worse. In 1927, as the great stock market boom was getting under way, it eased credit, an action to which I will return in the next chapter. This helped finance the stock market boom and thus made more severe the crash of 1929, although other factors were more important. After the Crash, during the great deflation of 1929 - 32, the Federal Reserve continued to worry about inflation. In these years banks were falling like the soldiers on that morning at the Somme. The Federal Reserve was indifferent to their fate, even to that of its own members. The idea of the lender of last resort had not crossed the Atlantic.

However, the prestige of the Federal Reserve remained undimmed. The head of the New York Federal Reserve Bank over much of this period was one Benjamin Strong; he was the first American central banker since Nicholas Biddle whose name was known. Strong owed his high reputation to the elegance of his errors. Men marveled that anyone should have the power to make such sophisticated mistakes. But this is an occupation where standards of performance are pleasantly relaxed. In central banking as in diplomacy, style, conservative tailoring and an easy association with the affluent count greatly and results for much less.

Gradually during the Depression interest rates were brought down; by 1931, the discount rate at the New York Reserve Bank — the rate at which banks could borrow — was 1.5 percent, hardly a usurious charge. The Federal Reserve also bought government bonds on a considerable scale, and the resulting cash went out to the banks — open market operations again. Soon the commercial banks were flush with lendable funds. All that remained was for customers to come to the banks, borrow money, increase deposits and enhance therewith the money supply. Recovery would then be prompt. Now came a terrible discovery. The customers wouldn't come. Even at the lowest rate they didn't think they could make money. The banks wouldn't trust those who were so foolish as to believe they could. That is how it was during the Depression. Cash simply accumulated in the banks; soon they had billions which they were able to lend but couldn't. The banking system had made worse the boom and made worse the crash. Now, when the Federal Reserve decided to act, nothing happened. Yet more remained to be learned about the management of money.

Irving Fisher

That such deficiency remained so late was not the fault of one of the two most interesting figures in the history of American economics. With Thorstein Veblen, whom we've already encountered, that was Irving Fisher. Both were students at Yale at nearly the same time in the last century.

Fisher, a neat, slender, handsome man with a patrician manner and a beautifully trimmed beard, was many things — a learned mathematician, a successful inventor, a disastrous speculator and a committed improver of the human race. He invented a simple card index system which he then manufactured himself and later sold at a handsome price to Remington Rand. His design for improving the race was by better nutrition and more thoughtful breeding — if horses, cattle and wheat, why not people? Also to improve the race, or anyhow its behavior, he was ardently for prohibition, although here economics entered. He argued, no doubt correctly, that men were more productive when off the sauce. In the late nineteen-twenties Fisher went heavily into the stock market and in the Crash lost between eight and ten million dollars. This was a sizable sum, even for an economics professor. When you read that the Consumers' Price Index has gone up, it is Fisher you have partly to thank. He pioneered in the development of index numbers and also in mathematical economics. Though mathematical economics has not yet taught us everything about the economy, it has proved a valuable way of keeping economists occupied.

Fisher's greatest contribution was to our understanding of money. He showed in one simple formula what determines its value. No one, however averse to mathematics, should be put off by it:

$$P = \frac{MV + M^1V^1}{T}$$

P is prices. M is the quantity of ordinary money or cash in circulation.

M¹ is also money, being that much larger part which consists of bank deposits. V and V¹ are the rate at which each of these two kinds is spent — their velocity of circulation. For centuries a relation had been recognized between prices and the supply of money. This was why prices rose with the issue of the Continental notes and the Greenbacks. Fisher's formula refined and made explicit this relationship. Prices go up as the amount of money, the M's, go up. But money is not merely hand-to-hand cash. Bank deposits subject to spending by check — M¹ — must be added. And, if money is quickly spent, the effect will obviously be greater than if it lies buried in a mattress or is a purely sedentary deposit in a bank. So quantity in each case is multiplied by rate of turnover — the respective V's or velocity of circulation. A particular increase in money supply will have more effect on prices if it is concentrated on a few transactions than if it is spread over many. So you divide by the number of transactions (the T in the equation) to allow for the volume of trade. That is all.

As a description of what determines the value of money, Fisher's equation of exchange is still accepted. Like πr^2, it may well endure.

For Irving Fisher, however, the equation was not merely a description of how things work; he thought it highly operational. By increasing or decreasing the supply of money, you could, he concluded, increase or decrease prices. By reducing or increasing prices, you could suppress the euphoria, offset the depression and thus moderate the cycle of speculation and disaster that had so long been such a blight on economic life. (Fisher was not the first to be captured by this thought.) With his formula in hand, he moved ahead on the remedy. He formed an association to promote the regulation of the money supply and thus to stabilize prices.

In the nineteen-thirties, prices being depressingly low, the obvious step was to increase the supply of money. Prices would then recover, business and employment would be stimulated. In 1933, his idea was adopted, more or less, by

Roosevelt. The gold content of the dollar was reduced; for the same gold there would be more dollars. It didn't work. The trial was not wholly fair, for the government kept most of the extra dollars. But Fisher's own formula showed why the effort failed. As money was created, people, frightened as they were in those Depression years, simply held on to it. Low velocity offset the increased quantity. More important, an increase in M, or hand-to-hand money, did not mean necessarily an increase in M^1, or bank deposits. These increased only as borrowers wanted to borrow, bankers wanted to lend. In the Depression, we have seen, neither borrowers nor bankers were willing. The supply of money could not be increased.

Fisher discovered what people, including numerous economists, have been exceedingly reluctant to believe. There are no cheap and easy inventions involving money alone that will solve all, or any, economic problems. Were it so, the inventions would already have been made; we would now all be saved from depression or inflation and be otherwise prosperous and happy.

But Irving Fisher's work was not wasted; it paved the way for a much more complex and imaginative step in economic policy. That was to have the government not only create money but also *ensure* its use — its velocity — by spending it. That was what Keynes now proposed. What is now called the Keynesian Revolution began with Irving Fisher. This Keynes himself affirmed. Writing to Fisher in 1944, he referred to him as one of his earliest teachers on these matters.

7.
The Mandarin Revolution

The ideas that made revolutions did not originate with the masses, with the people who, by any reasonable calculation, had the most reason for revolt. They came from intellectuals. This was noticed by Lenin: he thought intellectuals disputatious, perverse, undisciplined. But without them, he also believed, the armies of the proletariat would dissolve in purposeless confusion.

Those who are comfortable with things as they are, conservatives in the literal sense, have often and rightly been suspicious of intellectuals and have thought them troublemakers, unable to leave well enough alone, more reprehensible by any measure than the poor or discontented whom so unnecessarily they arouse. Intellectuals have usually thought themselves disliked because others were jealous of their brains. More often it's because they make trouble.

But intellectuals can render conservative as well as radical service. Before and after World War II, their ideas did much, for a time, to save the reputation of capitalism. As the ideas of socialism did not come from the masses, those that saved capitalism did not come from businessmen, bankers or owners of shares whose value had gone with the wind. They came principally from John Maynard Keynes. His fate was to be regarded as peculiarly dangerous by the class he rescued.

Cambridge, England

Keynes was born in 1883, the year that Karl Marx died. His mother, Florence Ada Keynes, a woman of high intelligence, was diligent in good works, a respected community leader and, in late life, the mayor of Cambridge. His father, John Neville Keynes, was an economist, logician and for some fifteen years the Registrary, which is to say the chief administrative officer of the University of Cambridge. Maynard, as he was always known to friends, went to Eton, where his first interest was in mathematics. Then he went to King's College, after Trinity the most prestigious of the Cambridge colleges and the one noted especially for its economists. Keynes was to add both to its prestige in economics and, as its bursar, to its wealth.

Churchill held — where I confess escapes me — that great men usually have unhappy childhoods. At both Eton and Cambridge, Keynes, by his own account and that of his contemporaries, was exceedingly happy. The point could be important. Keynes never sought to change the world out of any sense of personal dissatisfaction or discontent. Marx swore that the bourgeoisie would suffer for his poverty and his carbuncles. Keynes experienced neither poverty nor boils. For him the world was excellent.

While at King's, Keynes was one of a group of ardent young intellectuals which included Lytton Strachey, Leonard Woolf and Clive Bell. All, with wives — Virginia Woolf, Vanessa Bell — and lovers, would assemble later in London as the Bloomsbury Group. All were much under the influence of the philosopher, G. E. Moore. In later years Keynes told of what he had from Moore. It was the belief that: "The appropriate subjects of passionate contemplation and communion were a beloved person, beauty and truth, and one's prime objects in life were love, the creation and enjoyment of aesthetic experience and the pursuit of knowledge. Of these, love came a long way first."[1] With these thoughts, inevitably, Keynes found his interest shifting from mathematics to economics.

The more important instrument of the change was Alfred Marshall, who was not at King's but along the river in the equally beautiful precincts of St. John's, known as John's. Marshall, who combined the reputation of a prophet with the aura of a saint, presided over the world of Anglo-American economics in nearly undisputed eminence for forty years — from 1885 until his death in 1924. When I was first introduced to economics at Berkeley in 1931, it was Marshall's *Principles* students were required to read. It was a majestic book. It was also superb for discouraging second-rate scholars from any further pursuit of the subject.

When he finished with Cambridge in 1905, Keynes sat for the Civil Service examinations and did badly in economics. His explanation was characteristic: "The examiners presumably knew less than I did."[2] But this deficiency was not fatal, and he went to the India Office. Here he relieved his boredom by work on books — a technical treatise on the theory of probability and his later book on Indian currency. Neither much changed the world or economic thought; soon he returned to Cambridge on a fellowship provided personally by Alfred Marshall. It was the economics of Alfred Marshall — the notion, in particular, of a benign tendency to an equilibrium where all willing workers were employed — that Keynes would do most to make obsolete.

War and the Peace

When the Great War came, Keynes was not attracted to the trenches. He went to the Treasury, where his job was to take British earnings from trade, proceeds from loans floated in the United States and returns from securities conscripted and sold abroad and make them cover all possible overseas war purchases. And he helped the French and the Russians do the same. No magic was involved, as many have since suggested. Economic skill does not extend to getting very much for nothing. But an adept and resourceful mind was useful, and this Keynes had. In the course of time Keynes received a notice to report for military service. He sent it back. When the war was over, he was a natural choice for the British delegation to the Peace Conference. That, from the official view, was an appalling mistake.

The mood in Paris in the early months of 1919 was vengeful, myopic, indifferent to economic realities, and it horrified Keynes. So did his fellow civil servants.

So did the politicians. In June he resigned and came home, and, in the next two months, he composed the greatest polemical document of modern times. It was against the reparations clauses of the Treaty and, as he saw it, the Carthaginian peace.

Europe would only punish itself by exacting, or seeking to exact, more from the Germans than they had the practical capacity to pay. Restraint by the victors was not a matter of compassion but of elementary self-interest. The case was documented with figures and written with passion. In memorable passages Keynes gave his impressions of the men who were writing the peace. Woodrow Wilson he called "this blind and deaf Don Quixote."[3] Of Clemenceau he said: "He had one illusion — France; and one disillusion, mankind . . ."[4] On Lloyd George he was rather severe:

How can I convey to the reader, who does not know him, any just impression of this extraordinary figure of our time, this syren, this goat-footed bard, this half-human visitor to our age from the hag-ridden magic and enchanted woods of Celtic antiquity.[5]

Alas, no man is of perfect courage. Keynes deleted this passage on Lloyd George at the last moment.

The Economic Consequences of the Peace was published before the end of 1919. The judgment of the British Establishment was rendered by *The Times:* "Mr. Keynes may be a 'clever' economist. He may have been a useful Treasury official. But in writing this book, he has rendered the Allies a disservice for which their enemies will, doubtless, be grateful."[6] In time there would be a responsible view that Keynes went too far — that in calculating the limits on Germany's ability to pay, he was excessively orthodox. Perhaps he contributed to the Germans' sense of persecution and injustice that Hitler so effectively exploited. But the technique of *The Times* attack should also be noticed. It was not that the great men of the Treaty and the Establishment were suffering under the onslaught, although that, of course, was the real point. Rather, the criticism was causing rejoicing to the nation's enemies. It's a device to which highly respectable men regularly resort. "Even if you are right, it is only the Communists who will be pleased."

And it is when they are wrong that great men most resent the breaking of ranks. So they greatly resented Keynes. For the next twenty years he headed an insurance company and speculated in shares, commodities and foreign exchange, sometimes losing, more often winning. He also taught economics, wrote extensively and applied himself to the arts, old books and his Bloomsbury friends. But on public matters he was kept outside. He had broken the rules. We saw earlier that, as often as not, the intelligent man is not sought out. Rather, he is excluded as a threat.

Keynes's exclusion was his good fortune. The curse of the public man is that he first accommodates his tongue and eventually his thoughts to his public position. Presently saying nothing but saying it nicely becomes a habit. On the outside one can at least have the pleasure of inflicting the truth. Also, as a freelance intellectual, Keynes could marry Lydia Lopokova who had just enchanted London as the star of Diaghilev's ballet. My memory retains from somewhere a couplet:

> Was there ever such a union of
>   beauty and brains
> As when the lovely Lopokova
>   married John Maynard Keynes?

For a civil servant, even for a Cambridge professor, Lopokova would then have been a bit brave. As it was (according to legend), old family friends in Cambridge asked: has Maynard married a chorus girl?

Mostly in those years Keynes wrote. Good writing in economics is suspect — and with justification. It can persuade people. It also requires clear thought. No one can express well what he does not understand. So clear writing is perceived as a threat, something deeply damaging to the numerous scholars who shelter mediocrity of mind behind obscurity of prose. Keynes was a superb writer when he chose to try. This added appreciably to the suspicion with which he was regarded.

But while Keynes was kept outside, he could not, as would a Marxist, be ignored. He was a Fellow of King's. He was the Chairman of the National Mutual Insurance Company. He was the director of other companies. So he was heard. It might have been better strategy to have kept him inside and under control.

Churchill and Gold

The man who suffered most from Keynes's freedom from constraint was Winston Churchill. In 1925, Churchill presided over the most dramatically disastrous error by a government in modern economic history. It was Keynes who made it famous.

The mistake was the attempted return to the gold standard at the prewar gold and dollar value of the pound — 123.27 fine grains of gold and 4.86 dollars to the pound. Churchill was Chancellor of the Exchequer.

In retrospect, the error was not an especially subtle one. British prices and wages had risen during the war as they had in other countries. But in the United States they had risen less and fallen more in the postwar slump. And in France, as elsewhere in Europe, though prices had risen more than in Britain, the exchange value of the local currencies had fallen even more than prices had gone up. When you bought the cheap foreign currencies and then the goods, they were, in comparison with those of Britain, a bargain.

Had Britain gone back to the pound at, say, 4.40 dollars, all would have been well. With sterling bought at that rate, the cost of British commodities, manufactures or services — coal, textiles, machinery, ships, shipping — would have been pretty much in line with those of other countries, given their prices and the cost of their currencies. With pounds bought at 4.86 dollars, British prices were about 10 percent higher than those of her competitors. Ten percent is 10 percent. It was enough to send buyers to France, Germany, the Low Countries, the United States.

Why the mistake? To go back to the old rate of exchange of pounds for gold and dollars was to show that British financial management was again as solid, as reliable, as in the nineteenth century. It proved that the war had changed nothing. It was a thought to which Winston Churchill, historian and professional custodian of the British past, was highly susceptible. Also, only a few people participate in such decisions, and the instinct is strongly conformist. The man of greatest public prestige states his position at a meeting; the others hasten to praise his wisdom. Those who have a reputation for dissent, like Keynes, are not invited. They are not responsible, serious, effective. It follows that financial decisions, like those on foreign policy, are carefully orchestrated to protect error.

The country responded well to Churchill's House of Commons announcement of the return to gold. The

New York Times said in its headline that he had carried "PARLIAMENT AND NATION TO HEIGHT OF ENTHUSIASM." Keynes wrote instead to ask why Churchill did "such a silly thing." It was because he had "no instinctive judgment to prevent him from making mistakes."[7] And "lacking this instinctive judgment, he was deafened by the clamorous voices of conventional finance."[8] Also, he was misled by his experts. One cannot believe that Churchill read this exculpation with any pleasure.

If British exports were to continue, British prices had to come down. Prices could come down only if wages came down. And wages could come down in only one of two ways. There could be a horizontal slash, whatever the unions might say. Or there could be unemployment, enough unemployment to weaken union demands, threaten employed workers with idleness and thus bring down wages. This Keynes foresaw.

There was, in the end, both unemployment and a horizontal wage cut. As the mines of the Ruhr came back into production after 1924, world prices of coal fell. To meet this competition with the more expensive pound, the British coal-owners proposed a three-point program: longer hours in the pits, abolition of the minimum wage, lower wages for all. (Let Enoch Powell, Ronald Reagan and Milton Friedman take comfort; there was a day when such actions could be urged. Who knows, maybe their sun will shine again.) A Royal Commission agreed that the lower wage was necessary. The miners refused; the owners then locked them out. On the fourth of May, 1926, the transport, printing, iron and steel, electricity and gas and most of the building-trades unions came out in support of the miners. This, with some slight exaggeration, was called the General Strike. For quite a few workers it didn't make too much difference; they were already on the dole, for unemployment, the other remedy, was by then well advanced. In these years unemployment ranged between ten and twelve percent of the British labor force.

The General Strike lasted only nine days. Those who had most ardently applauded the return to gold were the first to see the strike as a threat to constitutional government, a manifestation of anarchy. Churchill took an especially principled stand. The miners remained on strike through most of 1926 but were eventually defeated. Keynes's judgment was redeemed but he was not forgiven. It had happened again: when the men of great reputation are wrong, it is the worst of personal tactics to be right.

The American Impact

After 1925, British prices remained stubbornly too high. Money that might have come to Britain for goods continued to go elsewhere, quite a lot to the United States and later to France. The return to gold was meant to proclaim the strength and integrity of sterling. It demonstrated its weakness and the strength of the dollar instead. In later years A. J. Liebling of *The New Yorker* magazine formulated what he called Liebling's Law. It held, roughly, that if a man of adequately complex mind proceeds in a sufficiently perverse way, he can succeed in kicking himself in his own ass out the door into the street. The return to gold in 1925 was a superb manifestation of Liebling's Law.

By 1927, the loss of gold to the United States was alarming. Accordingly, in that year, Montagu Norman, the head of the Bank of England, in company with Hjalmar Horace Greeley Schacht, the head of the Reichsbank (a man whose reputation for financial wizardry was supported by an exceptionally austere appearance and a notably frozen mind), sailed for New York to try and get it back. There, in company with Charles Rist of the Banque de France, they asked the Federal Reserve to lower its interest rate, expand its loans and thus ease monetary policy. The lower interest rates would discourage the flow of money to the United States. The easier money would mean more loans, more money, higher American prices, less competition in Britain and elsewhere from American goods and easier sales by Europeans in the United States. The Americans obliged. This was the action, as previously told that is held to have helped trigger the great stock market speculation of 1927 - 29. The easier money went to finance purchases of common stocks instead.

Everybody Ought to be Rich

The twenties were bad years in Britain, wonderful in the United States for everyone that counted. Farmers were very unhappy. Wages did not rise. But unemployment was low, industrial production rose, and so did profits and so, most of all, did the stock market. All common stocks rose during these years, and especially those that reflected the marvels of the new technology. Radio Corporation of America was the greatest speculative favorite — the electronic miracle, although that word had not yet come into use. For many investors Seaboard Airline was a foothold in the new world of aviation, although, in fact, it was a railroad.

Most exciting of all were the holding companies and the investment trusts. Both were companies formed to invest in other companies. And the companies in which they invested, invested in yet other companies that, in turn, invested in yet others. The layers could be five or ten deep. Along the way bonds and preferred stock were sold. The resulting interest payments and preferred dividends took some of the earnings of the ultimate operating company; the remaining earnings came cascading back to the common stock still held by the promoters. Or this happened as long as the dividends of the ultimate companies were good and rising. When these fell, the bond interest and preferred stock soaked up all of the revenues and more. Nothing was left to go upstream; the stock in the investment trusts and holding companies then went, often in a week, from wonderful to worthless. It was an eventuality that almost no one had foreseen.

The metaphor for all these promotions was Goldman Sachs. There had been nothing like it since the South Sea Bubble; there would be nothing like it again until I.O.S. (Investors Overseas Service) and Bernie Cornfeld.

The golden age of Goldman Sachs was the nearly eleven months beginning December 4, 1928. On that day the Goldman Sachs Trading Corporation was formed. This was an investment trust with the function only of investing in other companies; $100 million of stock was issued, of which 90 percent was sold to the public. This was put in other stock selected in accordance with the superior insights of Goldman Sachs. In February the Trading Corporation was merged with the Financial and Industrial Securities Corporation, another investment trust. Assets were now $235 million. In July the combined enterprise launched the Shenandoah Corporation. Preferred and common stocks to a total of $102.3 million were authorized, again for investment in other stock. The public share of issue was oversubscribed sevenfold so yet more was issued. In August Shenandoah, in turn, launched the Blue Ridge Corporation — for $142 million. A few days later, back at the Trading Corporation, $71.4 million more in securities was issued to buy another investment trust as well as a West Coast bank.

Shenandoah, which had been issued at $17.50 and had risen to $36.00, eventually went down to fifty cents. This was quite a loss. The Trading Corporation did worse. In February 1929, aided by some purchase of itself, it had reached $222.50. Two years later it could be had for a dollar or two. "He took my fortune," said one saddened commentator of his broker, "and ran it into a shoestring." A principal in this vast expropriation — a director of both Shenandoah and Blue Ridge — was John Foster Dulles. A more introspective man might have wondered. Dulles emerged with his faith in the capitalist system unshaken. We shall encounter him again.

Dark Thursday

For Goldman Sachs, as for stocks in general, the day of reckoning was Thursday, October 24, 1929. The market had been weak on the days before. On that morning, a story I've told before, there was a great unrestrained and unexplained headlong rush to sell. This hit the floor of the Exchange with torrential force. The machinery could not adjust to the panic. The ticker fell far behind the market. People across the country could not tell what was happening, only that they had been ruined or would soon be ruined. So they sold and were sold. Inside the Exchange the noise was deafening. Outside in Wall Street a crowd gathered. Perhaps capitalism was collapsing, which would be an interesting thing to see. The police were called; maybe the brokers and bankers would get out of hand. A workman appeared on one of the high buildings to make some repairs. The crowd assumed he was a suicide and waited impatiently for him to jump.

Around noon the Exchange authorities closed the visitors' gallery. It was all too obscene. One who had been watching was Winston Churchill. In the established if unduly simple view, his return to gold in 1925, the subsequent rescue of Britain by low interest rates and easy money in New York had been the cause of it all. It would be good to believe that it was design or guilt that had Churchill on hand but it isn't so. He only happened to be there.

About the time the gallery closed, things took a turn for the better. A little earlier that day the great New York bankers had gathered at Morgan's next door to consider the situation. A rescue operation seemed indicated. Richard Whitney, the Vice-President of the Exchange who was known to all as a Morgan broker, was told to go in and buy. This, with great ostentation, he did. The amounts authorized, though unknown, seem not to have been large. But the rescue worked, and the market turned dramatically around, although later in the day it became soft again. Whitney was a hero, his achievement was widely celebrated and he was made President of the Exchange. Not long thereafter, he was off to Sing Sing for embezzlement. The following Tuesday the real crash came. This time the bankers did not intervene. According to rumor they were unloading the stock they had bought the previous Thursday. With occasional rallies, the market went on down for nearly three years.

The Crash blighted consumer spending, business investment and the solvency of banks and business firms. After the Great Crash came the Great Depression; first the euthanasia of the rich, then of the poor. By 1933, nearly a fourth of all American workers were without jobs. Production — Gross National Product — was down by a third. As noted, around nine thousand banks failed. The government reacted normally: in June 1930, things were bad and getting much worse. A delegation called on President Hoover to ask for a public works relief program. He said: "Gentlemen, you have come sixty days too late. The depression is over."[9]

In Europe, it was World War I that shook the old certainties. The trenches would linger in social memory as the ultimate horror. In the United States it was the Great Depression. This remained in the American social memory for the next forty years and more. When anything seemed wrong, people would ask: "Does this mean another depression?"

Solutions

The effects of the Great Depression spread, and they spread around the world. The richer the country, the more advanced its industry, the worse, in general, the slump. Only Russia was untouched, although this was not an unqualified case for the Soviet system. The time had come for that further stage of the revolution that Lenin saw to be necessary so agriculture was being collectivized. This stage was infinitely more bloody than the first. What was called suffering in the West would have seemed like a miracle of economic affluence in Russia. Stalin himself was later to tell Churchill that these years were the most painful of his life. When Stalin was pained by the pain of others, it was pain indeed.

The first solution that occurred to statesmen was to propose tightening of belts, acceptance of hardship, resort to patience. This was a natural reaction. Few can believe that suffering, especially by others, is in vain. Anything that is disagreeable must surely have beneficial economic effects.

Herbert Hoover in the United States and Heinrich Brüning in Germany were the most devoted exponents of this view. Brüning's remedial action in 1931 was especially memorable. Wages were cut; prices were cut; salaries were cut; taxes were raised. All this was done at a time when around a quarter of all German industrial workers were unemployed. Not many have wanted to ask the question which some millions of German workers did ask themselves. If this is democracy, can Hitler be worse? Andrew Mellon, Hoover's Secretary of the Treasury, had a similar proposal: "Liquidate labor, liquidate stocks, liquidate the farmers . . ." After Mellon was finished, there would, it is true, be no way left but up.

Many economists — Lionel Robbins in England, Joseph Schumpeter in the United States — agreed that depression had a necessary, therapeutic function; the metaphor was that it extruded poisons that had been accumulating in the economic system. Others joined in urging patience, a course of action that is easier when supported by a regular income. And many warned that affirmative measures by government would cause inflation. The practical effect in all cases was to come out for inaction. It was not a good time for economists. Britain did abandon the gold standard and free trade. Otherwise Westminster and Whitehall reacted to the Depression by ignoring the steady flow of advice it was receiving from John Maynard Keynes.

Keynes was wholly clear as to the proper action. He wanted borrowing by the government and the expenditure of the resulting funds. This was the essential step on from Irving Fisher. The borrowing ensured the increase in the money supply — in bank deposits or Fisher's famous M^1. What was spent was spent by the government and would then be respent by workers and others receiving the money. The government spending and the further spending by the recipients ensured that there would be no offsetting drop in velocity — in V and V^1. You not only created money but enforced its use.

Keynes in these years did have one

notable friend. It was the "goat-footed bard," David Lloyd George. Keynes explained helpfully that he supported Lloyd George when he was right and opposed him when he was wrong. But Lloyd George was by now in the political wilderness with the other winners and losers from World War I. Gradually for Keynes there was compensation. He became a prophet with honor except in his own country. The most successful application of his policies was, in fact, where he was all but unknown.

The Trial Runs

The Nazis were not given to books. Their reaction was to circumstance, and this served them better than the sound economists served Britain and the United States. From 1933, Hitler borrowed money and spent — and he did it liberally as Keynes would have advised. It seemed the obvious thing to do, given the unemployment. At first, the spending was mostly for civilian works — railroads, canals, public buildings, the *Autobahnen*.

Exchange control then kept frightened Germans from sending their money abroad and those with rising incomes from spending too much of it on imports.

The results were all a Keynesian could have wished. By late 1935, unemployment was at an end in Germany. By 1936, high income was pulling up prices or making it possible to raise them. Likewise wages were beginning to rise. So a ceiling was put over both prices and wages, and this too worked. Germany, by the late thirties, had full employment at stable prices. It was, in the industrial world, an absolutely unique achievement.

The German example was instructive but not persuasive. British and American conservatives looked at the Nazi financial heresies — the borrowing and spending — and uniformly predicted a breakdown. Only Schacht, the banker, they said, was keeping things patched together. (They did not know that Schacht, so far as he was aware of what was happening, was opposed.) And American liberals and British socialists looked at the repression, the destruction of the unions, the

Brownshirts, the Blackshirts, the concentration camps, the screaming oratory, and ignored the economics. Nothing good, not even full employment, could come from Hitler. It was the American case that was influential.

At the close of 1933, Keynes addressed a letter to Franklin D. Roosevelt, which, not seeking reticence, he published in the *New York Times*. A single sentence summarized his case: "I lay overwhelming emphasis on the increase of national purchasing power resulting from governmental expenditure which is financed by loans. . . ."[10] The following year he visited FDR but the letter had been a better means of communication. Each man was puzzled by the face-to-face encounter. The President thought Keynes some kind of "a mathematician rather than a political economist."[11] Keynes was depressed; he had "supposed the President was more literate, economically speaking."[12]

If corporations are large and strong, as they already were in the thirties, they can reduce their prices. And if unions are nonexistent or weak, as they were at the time in the United States, labor can then be forced to accept wage reductions. Action by one company will force action by another. The modern inflationary spiral will work in reverse; the reduced purchasing power of workers will add to its force. Through the National Recovery Admnistration Washington was trying to arrest this process — a reasonable and even wise effort, given the circumstances. This Keynes and most economists did not see; he and they believed the NRA wrong, and ever since it has had a poor press. One of FDR's foolish mistakes. Keynes wanted much more vigorous borrowing and spending; he thought the Administration far too cautious. And Washington was, indeed, reluctant.

In the early thirties the Mayor of New York was James J. Walker. Defending a casual attitude toward dirty literature, as it was then called, he said he had never heard of a girl being seduced by a book. Keynes was now, after a fashion, to prove Walker wrong. Having failed by direct, practical persuasion, he proceeded to seduce Washington and the world by way of a book. Further to prove the point against Walker, it was a nearly unreadable one.

The General Theory

The book was *The General Theory of Employment Interest and Money*. (For some reason Keynes omitted the commas.) He at least was not in doubt about its influence. Shortly before it was published in 1936, he told George Bernard Shaw that it would "largely revolutionise . . . the way the world thinks about economic problems."[13] So it did.

The General Theory was published long before it was finished. Like the Bible and *Das Kapital,* it is deeply ambiguous and, as in the case of the Bible and Marx, the ambiguity helped greatly to win converts. I'm not reaching for paradox. When understanding is achieved after much effort, readers hold tenaciously to their belief. The pain, they wish to think, was worthwhile. And if there are enough contradictions and ambiguities, as there

370

are also in the Bible and Marx, the reader can always find something he wants to believe. This too wins disciples.

Keynes's basic conclusion can, however, be put very directly. Previously it had been held that the economic system, any capitalist system, found its equilibrium at full employment. Left to itself, it was thus that it came to rest. Idle men and idle plant were an aberration, a wholly temporary failing. Keynes showed that the modern economy could as well find its equilibrium with continuing, serious unemployment. Its perfectly normal tendency was to what economists have since come to call an underemployment equilibrium.

The ultimate cause of the underemployment equilibrium lay in the effort by individuals and firms to save more from income than it was currently profitable for businessmen to invest. What is saved from income must ultimately be spent or there will be a shortage of purchasing power. Previously for 150 years such a possibility had been excluded in the established economics. The income from producing goods was held always to be sufficient to buy the goods. Savings were always invested. Were there a surplus of savings, interest rates fell, and this ensured their use.

Keynes did not deny that all savings got invested. But he showed that this could be accomplished by a fall in output (and employment) in the economy as a whole. Such a slump reduced earnings, changed business gains into losses, reduced personal incomes, and, while it reduced investment, it reduced savings even more. It was in this way that savings were kept equal to investment. Adjustment, a benign word in economics, could be a chilling thing.

From the foregoing came the remedy. The government should borrow and invest. If it borrowed and invested enough, all savings would be offset by investment at a high, not a low, level of output and employment. *The General Theory* validated the remedy that Keynes had previously urged. It would have been inconvenient if it had come out the other way.

The University Route

Washington, as noted, was cool to Keynes. So, with *The General Theory* as his weapon, he captured the United States by way of the universities. His principal point of entry was Harvard. It was something I was fortunate enough to see at first hand. I was living as a young tutor at Winthrop House, one of the undergraduate residence units. Winthrop House was an unpretentious place, slightly anti-Semitic like the rest of the university but not anti-Irish as were the more dignified places of residence. It was perhaps for this reason that among our inhabitants were the Kennedy brothers, something that had a considerable effect on my later life.

Resident tutors had free rooms, free meals and as much money as they needed. We met each morning for a leisurely breakfast and to hear of the exceptionally depraved sexual adventures of one of our colleagues on the previous night. He subsequently became a very great social scientist. It was a lovely and tranquil world; the only drawback was that things were so different just outside the university walls. Once in those Depression years I spent Christmas in Los Angeles. The streets were filled with desperate men who pled desperately for a little money; you could sense that they hated what they had to do but they had no choice. When you tried to pass them by, you saw the look of hopelessness and fright in their eyes. That was the contrast with our comfortable world.

Keynes had a solution without revolution. Our pleasant world would remain; the unemployment and suffering would go. It seemed a miracle. In 1936, after the publication of *The General Theory,* there were meetings several times a week to discuss this wonderful thing. One meeting in Winthrop House remains in my memory. Professor Schumpeter presided; he disliked Keynes but loved argument more. Robert Bryce, a brilliant young Canadian, had just come from Keynes's seminar in the other Cambridge, as it was called. When in doubt, as we often were, he told us what Keynes really meant. For the next thirty years Bryce was the pre-eminent figure in Canadian economic policy. More than anyone else he caused Canada to become, even before the United States or Britain, a pillar of the Keynesian faith.

It was the young who were captured. Economists are economical, among other things, of ideas. It is still so. They make those they acquire as graduate students do for a lifetime. Change in economics comes only with the changing generations. The great economists of that day read and reviewed Keynes and uniformly found him wrong.

But so influential was Keynes among the young at Harvard that in later years an association of alumni was formed to combat his influence. They threatened to cease financial support to the university unless his ideas were repressed or expunged, although it is not clear that many had given much before. Conservatives regularly extend their faith to the management of their personal resources. I was singled out for attack as the Crown Prince of "Keynesism." I was greatly pleased and hoped that my friends would be properly resentful.

That was Keynes. You came to him out of conservatism, your desire for peaceful change. And by urging his ideas you won a reputation for being a radical.

To Washington

From Harvard the ideas of Keynes went to Washington — by train. On Thursday and Friday nights in the New Deal years the Federal Express out of Boston to Washington would be half-filled with Harvard faculty members, old and young. All were on the way to impart wisdom to the New Deal. The *Harvard Crimson* once said of the lectures of a noted professor of government that they were what he gave while catching the train to Washington. After *The General Theory* was published, the wisdom that the younger economists sought to impart was that of Keynes.

It was thus that we learned of the Washington reluctance. To spend public money to create jobs might be necessary. But it was not something you urged out of choice. And to urge that a budget deficit was a *good* thing in itself — the heart of the Keynesian remedy — seemed insane. Men of sound judgment were repelled. Even one's best friends, if in positions of responsibility, were cautious in the presence of such heresy. One does not overcome such caution by logic or eloquence but almost always the opposition comes to your rescue. It came galloping in those years.

In 1937, recovery from the Great Depression was slowly under way; production and prices were rising, although unemployment was still appalling. The men of sound judgment now asserted themselves. They moved to cut spending, raise taxes and bring the federal budget into balance. The few Keynesians protested; our voices were drowned out in the roars of orthodox applause. As the budget moved toward balance, the recovery came to a halt. Presently there was a new and ghastly slump, a recession within the Depression. It was entirely as Keynes predicted. The men of sound judgment had made our case.

The American Keynesians

Where were our allies in Washington? They were, of all places, in the Federal Reserve System. We think of a central bank as a stronghold of myopic, unyielding conservatism. It is not an extravagant view but the Federal Reserve was then headed by Marriner Eccles, a Utah banker of highly original mind. Eccles had seen the lines of depositors form outside his own banks to get their money. He had seen men looking without hope for work. He knew the worried, broken farmers outside town. Why not have the government spend money to provide jobs and help the farmers back to solvency? His experience had caused ideas very similar to those of Keynes to pass through his mind. Roosevelt had brought him to Washington.

Eccles's principal economic aide was Lauchlin Currie, another of the notable Canadians who, in their selfless way, had come south to rescue the Republic. Previously he had been a faculty member at Harvard and had published a book on the supply and control of money that had anticipated some of the important propositions of Keynes. This caused him to be viewed with doubt by the great economists, and he was not promoted. In economics one should never be right too soon. The shrewd scholar always waits until the parade is passing his door and then steps bravely out in front of the band. Eccles and Currie became the leading exponents of Keynes in Washington.

Scholars now speak of the Keynesian Revolution. Never before had a revolution captured a country by way of a bank. No one should worry that it will happen often again.

From the Federal Reserve in the late thirties Currie went to the White House as an assistant to FDR. This was a strategic spot. When an economic post opened in the government or someone was needed for a special economic task, he would see, if possible, that someone with reliably Keynesian views was employed. Several times he called on me. Conservatives always believed that there was a conspiracy to promote the Keynesian ideas. This everyone concerned indignantly denied. Much depends on the point of view. In later years Currie was accused of being a Communist. He was not. But for many people the difference between Keynes and Communism wasn't too great.

Also in the latter thirties, Keynes won his most important influential American recruit; that was Alvin Harvey Hansen, a professor first at Minnesota and then at Harvard and one of the most prestigious figures in the American economic pantheon. Hansen was no youngster whose views could be dismissed by the economic establishment. In books, articles and through his students he propagated the faith. Hansen and two other scholars — Seymour E. Harris, another diligent evangelist at Harvard, and Paul M. Samuelson, whose textbook, in face of sharp initial attack, instructed millions — made Keynes an accepted part of American economic thought.

Although the recession of 1937 made Keynes's ideas respectable in Washington, action to lift the level of employment remained half-hearted. In 1939, the year war came to Europe, nine and a half million Americans were unemployed. That was 17 percent of the labor force. Almost as many (14.6 percent) were still unemployed the following year.

The war then brought the Keynesian remedy with a rush. Expenditures doubled and redoubled. So did the deficit. Before the end of 1942, unemployment was minimal. In many places labor was scarce.

There is another way of looking at this history. Hitler, having ended unemployment in Germany, had gone on to end it for his enemies. He was the true protagonist of the Keynesian ideas.

Lessons of War

The war revealed two of the enduring features of the Keynesian Revolution. One was the moral difference between spending for welfare and spending for war. During the Depression very modest outlays for the unemployed seemed socially debilitating, economically unsound. Now expenditures many times greater for weapons and soldiers were perfectly safe. It's a difference that still persists.

Also as unemployment diminished, but well before it disappeared, inflation became a threat. Keynes believed himself to have a remedy and so did his followers; it was to put everything into reverse. Raise taxes to keep pace with wartime spending, thus try by all possible means to keep down the budget deficit. Keep the cost of living stable, if necessary by subsidizing the cost of food and other staples. Labor could then be asked to forgo wage increases for the duration. Some price control and rationing might be necessary; it should be applied selectively to essentials in especially short supply. Keynes set it all out in a famous series of letters to *The Times*. In Washington and by now in London the proposals were widely accepted. If Keynes said so, it must surely work.

I circulated a paper with a similar set of proposals in Washington to which I'd been summoned by Lauchlin Currie. It was an inspired action, for, as a consequence, in the spring of 1941, I was put in charge of price control, one of the most powerful economic positions of the wartime years. To say I was overjoyed would be a gross understatement.

I got the news in the Blaine Mansion, a fine Victorian structure on Massachusetts Avenue at Dupont Circle and the first headquarters for wartime price control. James Blaine, like many others, achieved a well-deserved obscurity by running unsuccessfully for the presidency. But his obscurity is less complete than for most. A verse from the campaign, simple, forthright, good in scan and rhyme, survives to celebrate his character and provenance:

James G. Blaine, James G. Blaine,
Continental liar from the State of Maine.

In a few weeks we outgrew the Blaine house. Three times during the war we burst at the housing seams and had to move. We ended in a sizable acreage previously inhabited by the Census and later taken over by the FBI. The expansion in staff was related to the deeper discovery that, for inflation, the ideas of Keynes as adapted by Galbraith did not work. Long before all the unemployed had jobs, corporations could raise prices — and they did. This led, in turn, to wage demands and on, potentially, to a price-wage spiral. Meanwhile taxes could not be raised fast enough to keep pace with wartime spending. The excess of purchasing power could not, as Keynes had proposed, be mopped up.

The only hope was to go in for price-fixing on a vast scale. This, in the spring of 1942, we did, and rationing followed. That policy did work; prices were kept nearly stable throughout the war.

Previously I had argued against a general ceiling on prices with great conviction; now I argued for it with equal passion. Almost no one noticed this change of mind. No one at all criticized it. In economics it is a far, far wiser thing to be right than to be consistent.

A revisionist view, greatly favored by partisans of the free market, now holds that price increases were only bottled up, to be released after the war. There was, indeed, a bulge when the controls were lifted in 1946, but it was less by far than the increase in the single peacetime year of 1974. Without the controls prices before the war's end would have been doubling and redoubling every year.

With minor exceptions we eventually had control of all the prices in the United States. There could be appeal to higher authority and the courts. No one much did, for higher authority backed us up. If anyone left our offices with a smile, we felt we had not done our job. To be effective, price control had to be painful. To be charged with inflicting such pain, mostly on those who could handsomely afford it, was a psychologically damaging experience for a young man. I was accused of liking it, which, perhaps, I did.

People appealing for price increases came to a large table in the Census Building. Those with the worst case always made the most compelling plea. Knowing that their case was fraudulent, they had rehearsed with the greatest care at the greatest length. We usually had the figures on their earnings; I would look down the row of chairs while someone was pleading his meretricious case and notice that one or more staff members would have a hand resting flat on the table, the index and second fingers moving up and down, each in opposite direction to the other. It was in reference to a fable — the year of the great famine in the land of the ants. One day a patrol from an ant colony on the side of a steep hill found food, a lovely large, round piece of horse manure. It was directly up the slope from the colony. All the ants were mustered out to bring back the food. They rolled it down the hill, and presently it was rolling faster and faster and threatening to roll right by the ant colony and be lost. The queen ant went up and down the lines encouraging her troops, who were holding against the food, to ever greater exertions. Her antennae were going up and down like the fingers. In ant language it meant, "Stop that horse-shit."

It was while directing price control that I first met Keynes. I had gone to study under him at Cambridge — Cambridge,

England, of course — in 1937 - 38, but it was then that he had his first heart attack, and he did not appear at the university at al that year. He came into my outer office in Washington unannounced one day to deliver a paper. My secretary brought it in and said he seemed to feel he should see me. The name, she said, was Kines. I looked at the paper; there it was, *J. M. Keynes.* The paper was a lucid condemnation of the prices we were setting on corn and hogs. He called them maize and pigs. It was as though St. Peter had dropped in on some parish priest.

With much more emphasis on rationing and less on price control, the British economic policy during the war was otherwise similar to ours. There too it worked. British wartime planning got more from less than that of any other country. As the war ended, I led a group of economists who studied German and Japanese wartime economic management. None doubted that the British management was far more rigorous.

Triumph

After 1941, the economists no longer went to Washington by train. They were already there. All saw the Keynesian remedy for depression and unemployment from, as it were, the front row. The conclusion was inescapable: what would work in war would work in peace. The Keynesian victory was now assured. The failure of the Keynesian system to deal with inflation was not stressed. Inflation was surely peculiar to the war.

Liberal businessmen in these years began to show interest; they formed the Committee for Economic Development to promote the ideas. They were very careful, however, to avoid Keynes's name. And they spoke not of deficits but of a budget balanced only at a high level of employment.

As the war drew to a close, a group of young economists decided to seek Congressional sanction for the idea of government planning to maintain employment. They succeeded, and the Employment Act of 1946 became law. I was one of the many who were surprised at their success. I had thought the idea premature and had not participated in the effort. But, by 1946, it was becoming difficult even for conservative Republicans (or Democrats) to be against full employment, although, in the end, many did rise to the challenge.

Bretton Woods

Meanwhile Keynes himself was completing his last crusade. At Paris he had fought the Carthaginian peace. In 1925, he had fought Churchill and the tyranny of gold. In 1944, representatives from 44 countries had assembled at Bretton Woods in New Hampshire to ensure that the errors on gold and reparations on which Keynes had made his reputation were not repeated. The Bretton Woods Conference was not a conference among nations. It was a conference of nations with Keynes. His only rival was Harry D. White, his friend and disciple at the U.S. Treasury. The result of Bretton Woods was the Bank for International Reconstruction and

Development and the International Monetary Fund. The first would guide the minds of the victorious powers to reconstruction, not punishment. The second would give a modicum of flexibility to the rule of gold. A country in trouble could win time by borrowing from the fund.

When the war was over, Keynes also negotiated the loan — $3.75 billion — that was to see Britain through the postwar years and until exports would again pay for imports. There was now another terrible aberration of the orthodox financial mind — this time it was the Americans. Sterling had been subject to rigid exchange controls during the war. It was made a condition of the loan that it would become fully and freely convertible into dollars (and thus into gold) according to timetable in 1947. This was done. And all who had accumulated wartime hoards of inconvertible sterling — speculators, black-market currency operators, the banks — rushed joyously to change their money into dollars. The loan was used up, literally in a matter of days. In 1925, sterling had been made convertible at an unduly high rate with disastrous results. Twenty-two years later the same error was repeated with infinite precision. This time Keynes was a reluctant participant.

Keynes had always believed that men of self-confessed financial wisdom were wonderfully consistent, especially in their mistakes. He did not live to see this further proof. On April 21, 1946, he died of another heart attack.

The Age of Keynes

After the fiasco of the British loan came the Marshall Plan. This took a far more practical view of the postwar world; with it Europe recovered. The Marshall Plan was a good example of the kind of concerted effort backed by money that Keynes had called for at Bretton Woods.

Germany was a full participant in the Marshall aid. This too was the legacy of Keynes. In the years after 1945, men told each other there must, on no account, be another harsh peace. Keynes's philippic against the Versailles Treaty was now the conventional wisdom. A defeated enemy was now helped, not punished.

In Europe and the United States the two decades following the Second World War will for long be remembered as a very good time, the time when capitalism really worked. Everywhere in the industrialized countries production increased. Unemployment was everywhere low. Prices were nearly stable. When production lagged and unemployment rose, governments intervened to take up the slack, as Keynes had urged. So these were good and confident years, a good time to be an economist, and economists took and were given credit for the achievement. Only the occasional, very mild recessions were still acts of nature or of God.

But these years showed the flaws in the Keynesian miracle as well, although the faults were less celebrated. After the Marshall Plan there was hope that a similar infusion of money — capital — would also rescue the poor countries from their poverty. The rich countries weren't overwhelming in their generosity. But enough was done to show the problem.

In the European countries in the years immediately following the war capital was the missing ingredient. This could be provided and was provided by the Marshall Plan. In the poor countries, on the other hand, industrial experience, industrial skill, industrial discipline, effective public administration, transportation systems and many other things did not exist. These could not be supplied from abroad as was the capital. Nor could anything be done from abroad about the relentless pressure of population on land. Keynes, it was learned, at least by some, was a man for the rich countries, not the poor.

And the great lesson of the war was rediscovered. The Keynesian remedy was asymmetrical; it would work against unemployment and depression but not in reverse against inflation. It was a discovery that was only very slowly and reluctantly accepted, and now, more than thirty years later, there are still some followers of the master who are reluctant to admit the fault. Unemployment, as this is written, is high — in the United States the highest in thirty years. And industrial prices are going steadily, steadily up. What is true in the United States is worse in Britain. But Keynes, once a heretic, is now the prophet of the established faith. One must believe that for his remedies to work.

Inflation can be cured by having enough unemployment. However, with this cure no Keynesian can agree; the essence of the Keynesian system is that it cures unemployment. One can stop the increase in corporate prices and trade-union wages by direct action. (I've long thought such action inescapable.) This does not leave the market system intact as Keynes, the conservative, had intended. It is a portent of radical change that not many wish to face.

There are other problems. Keynesian support to the economy has come to involve heavy spending for arms. This, we've seen, is blessed as sound while spending for welfare and the poor is always thought dangerous. With time, too, it has become evident that Keynesian progress can be an uneven thing: many automobiles, too few houses; many cigarettes, too little health care. The great cities in trouble. As these problems have obtruded, the confident years have come to an end. The Age of Keynes was for a time but not for all time.

8.
The Fatal Competition

[The American people must be on] guard against the acquisition of unwarranted influence, whether sought or unsought, by the military-industrial complex. The potential for the disastrous rise of misplaced power exists and will persist . . . We should take nothing for granted.
— President Dwight D. Eisenhower, 1961

To understand this world you must know that the military establishments of the United States and the Soviet Union have united against the civilians of both countries.
— A high official of the Department of State to the author, 1974

In his testimony today, Mr. Haughton refused to characterize the payments [to other governments] as bribes, explaining that one of his lawyers . . . preferred to call them "kickbacks."

"If you get the contract," Mr. Haughton said, "it's pretty good evidence that the payments had to be made."
— From the *New York Times* account of the testimony of Daniel J. Haughton, Chairman of the Lockheed Aircraft Corporation, before the Senate Banking and Currency Committee, August 25, 1975

Politics, in one of the oldest of professional clichés, is the art of the possible. Equally, in its highest development, it is the art of separating the important from the peripheral and then concentrating on what is important, no matter how difficult. No problem in our time is a fraction so important, no source of uncertainty a fraction so valid as the arms competition between the United States and the Soviet

Union. This competition has now developed the means for mutual and reciprocal destruction of the two nations, along with the rest of the world, in a matter of hours. Vast technical resources are being invested in the effort to reduce this to minutes. We are concerned in these pages with the ideas that explain our society and guide our behavior. What doctrine and circumstance lie back of this awful effort? There is nothing else that could be so important.

The competition just mentioned rests on two broad currents of thought, both exceptionally ominous in their implications. First, there is the concept of conflict — irreconcilable conflict — between inherently hostile economic, political and social systems. There can be no reconciliation between Communism and capitalism, authoritarian discipline and personal liberty, atheism and spiritual faith. That is the great fact of life.

The second and more recent idea is explicit in the words above of President Eisenhower and the nameless State Department official, only slightly less so in the response of Mr. Daniel Haughton, the since-deposed head of Lockheed. It holds that the arms race is the result of the way we are ruled. It is a manifestation, both in the United States and in the Soviet Union, of the public power of the military establishment and of those who make the arms. It involves a double symbiosis. In the United States the great weapons firms supply the armed services with the weapons they seek. The Air Force, Navy and Army reciprocate with the orders to the corporations that provide the profits and employment by which they function and flourish. The corporations and the services combine to conduct the research and development which make the current generation of arms obsolete and make necessary the next.

This is the first symbiosis. The second is between the United States and the Soviet Union. The same process in only slightly different form exists there. Each power, by its innovations and acquisitions, then creates the need and incentive for the other power to do the same — or more. Thus each works with the other to ensure that the competition is self-perpetuating. The difference between Communism and capitalism, freedom and authority, progress and reaction, Marx and Jesus, is cited but this is liturgical, not real. No faith sustains the arms competition. All who are knowledgeable agree that neither system would survive the conflict. Both countries are caught in a squirrel wheel, a trap.

There are many ways in which the history of the last thirty years could be written. I see no part of that history as so important as the changing vision of the arms race, from its perception as a conflict between systems to the present tendency to view it as a web of power by which we are ensnared. We are all greatly the product of our education in these matters. Mine began in Berlin very soon after the end of World War II.

Berlin: 1945

I knew Berlin rather well before the war; I went there in 1938 to study Hitler's land and agricultural policy. I had just learned that, in academic life, the selection of improbable subjects of study involving extensive travel is taken to suggest an imaginative and inquiring mind and is also a relief from tedium. My next glimpse of the great city was in the summer of 1945. One thought of the landscape of the moon; this was a phrase that came to many lips. When eventually we saw the landscape of the moon, it was more austere and chaste, less broken and much less alarming than Berlin in those summer days.

In 1945, Berlin was literally a city of death, for the bodies were still in the canals and tunnels and under the broken buildings. From Tempelhof airdrome where you came in, one saw burial parties passing into the big cemetery nearby, and also American soldiers with their girls. As a civilian, I had not previously realized that an accomplished warrior could make love with an M-1 rifle slung on his shoulder. Life in Berlin went on.

Half-destroyed buildings are the metaphor of the suffering that goes with war. The experience of horror is by people. But its image does not persist; very soon it cannot be seen at all. Only in structures does it endure. In Nazi times the Haus Vaterland was a famous conglomerate of restaurants and cabarets. Each of the different watering places featured the music, costumes, food and alcohol of a different part of the Reich. In 1945, most of Berlin was a metaphor of destruction. Today the visitor must search out the Haus Vaterland in a wilderness near the Wall to see how the horror of war endures.

In the summer of 1945, I was at a headquarters near Frankfurt with a group that was assessing the effects of the air attacks on the German war economy. One morning one of my fellow directors of the enterprise, George Ball — later Under Secretary of State, Ambassador to the United Nations, a banker and much else — called to remind me that the Big Three — Churchill, Stalin, Truman — would soon be meeting at Potsdam to decide the future of Germany and the world. He thought we should attend. I noted, as a difficulty, that we hadn't been invited.

George said that to allow hurt feelings to keep us away would only compound that error. So we flew to Berlin in an old C-47 we'd been given for our work, were admitted immediately to the conference compound on our word that we had come to participate and began operations with an excellent lunch at the senior officials' mess. I was immediately made welcome by the committee that was considering reparations policy; its chairman, Isador Lubin, was an old friend. Ever since, I've wondered how many attending the great summit conferences were self-invited volunteers. In the following months I was concerned with German matters; eventually, in the State Department, I was put in charge of economic affairs in the occupied countries. (There is a lesson here: reticence and modesty ought not to stand in the way of public service.) These responsibilities brought me back to Berlin.

Soldiers, businessmen, civil servants, diplomats, assorted idlers and black marketeers were gathered in the city for the tasks of the occupation. By 1946, two parties were taking form: one party wanted very much to get along with the Russians. They — I should say we, for I was among them — saw little hope for a world in which there was conflict between the two powers. There were things to encourage us. When we met socially with the Russians, we learned how grim had been their experience with war, how passionate was their fear of another. Some of our senior army people were similarly moved. They had experienced war and wanted no more of it. We had as symbolic allies our enlisted men. They were meeting regularly with their Russian counterparts for the sale and exchange of merchandise; the market was in the shadow of the Brandenburg Gate which stands between East and West Berlin. Thus they showed that trade was above ideology, that when the armed representatives of capitalism met the armed might of Communism, the natural tendency was not to fight but to do a little business.

There was a second party. It regarded our hopes as ridiculously soft-headed. (There is an interesting point here: political wisdom is thought always to lie with the hard, impervious head and the tough, unyielding mind. One wonders why.) Some members of this group were only concerned to show how tough and hence how intelligent they were. But some, the Foreign Service Officers especially, spoke out of a genuine knowledge of Stalin and the great purges and a genuine concern for his intentions. Also the Soviet activities in Eastern Europe left no room for doubt. It was easy to assume that these would be the same in Western Europe as well.

Present too were the pathologically belligerent, those who even more than the poor are always with us. And there were a few for whom the war had been an exciting thing, a blessed escape from dull jobs, dull wives, deadly routine. Better another war than going back to Toledo, Ohio, or Nashua, New Hampshire.

On occasion, the debate became rather intense. We met in the late afternoons and evenings in the houses of the former Nazis and the German bourgeoisie. The bombs had wrecked the working and middle-class sections of Berlin but largely spared the affluent suburbs. Now the rich had their turn. They were summarily evicted to make way for those who were guiding the occupation. Not many of the latter had ever been housed so well before. All visitors to Berlin remarked on how easily and graciously Americans accommodated to the management of a complement of servants.

In these rather grand surroundings the talk turned regularly to Marx and Lenin. Not all who spoke of their design remembered much of their texts but they were confident of their purpose. It was world revolution, a world Communist order. Everyone in Berlin was a potential hostage to this effort.

The Bureaucratic Interest

These were the heroic thoughts. There was a deeper practical interest. The war had brought great prestige and influence to the armed forces. It had also done wonders for American business. In the previous Depression years businessmen, along with the banks, had been a favorite target of abuse. Then, during the war, the achievement in increasing production and supplying arms had been excellent. Profits had also been good. And a new and close relationship between industry and the armed services had been forged.

This was the beginning of the political alignment, the symbiosis of which I earlier spoke. The Air Force, in particular, had expanded wonderfully in power, prestige, men and airplanes. And a whole new industry had come into existence to provide the equipment and technology and share the gains. There followed a very simple, very practical point, far too obvious to be ignored. If there were a continuing menace, these gains would be continued. If not, they would be lost. The Soviets, not the French, not the British, not the Germans, were obvious candidates to be the new menace.

No one — certainly not many — argued that the gains of war should be preserved by the invention of a new menace. This is not the kind of thing that is said openly; the world has little to fear from forthrightly cynical men. Not many admitted this motivation even to themselves. Personal interest always wears the disguise of public purpose, and no one is more easily persuaded of the validity or righteousness of a public cause than the person who stands personally to gain therefrom. Those who perceive the underlying role of self-interest often hesitate to cite it. Nothing so interrupts the flow of polite conversation and so badly repays an invitation to drink and dine.

The doctrine of inevitable conflict had on its side the businessmen but there were others. It pleases the slightly insecure intellectual to agree with a down-to-earth man of affairs or a general. He proves to himself that he too can function in the world of practical action.

One felt, as time passed, that the practical and respectable men would prevail. So they did.

The Blockade

But one cannot discount the support the doctrine of inevitable conflict had from the Soviets. This, intended or otherwise, was comprehensive and superbly timed. In 1948, land and water communications with Berlin through the Soviet zone were interrupted. The barriers were closed. The ostensible cause was the currency reform in West Germany and its application to West Berlin. But, as read, the Soviet intention was to force the Allies out of Berlin. An heroic gesture was called for; it would be shown that a great city could be supplied, if necessary, entirely through the air. There followed the Berlin airlift.

Time has altered the earlier view of this event. The Soviets were certainly seeking to harass, discourage and protest. Not many historians now think they were seeking a final showdown. They may well have been surprised by the reaction. General Lucius Clay, the American commander at the time, has always believed that an Allied convoy presenting itself firmly at the checkpoints would have been let through.

But we had airplanes. Having air power, air power must be a solution. More often than imagined, this has been the basis of military policy. However, it is not easy to criticize men who wished, at whatever cost, to minimize the risk of the armed confrontation that the airlift seemed to avoid. I do not do so. By the spring of 1949, eight thousand tons of freight were being landed each day in Berlin by the primitive piston planes of the time. That was enough, though barely, to sustain the life of the city.

Then agreement was reached, communications were resumed, the airlift came to an end. Coal, the principal cargo, had for a brief moment enjoyed the prestige of air passage; now it was returned to the trains and barges. But by this time a further chain of events was proclaiming the inevitability of conflict. In May 1948, Communist power was fully consolidated in Czechoslovakia. By the end of 1949, the Communist victory was complete in China. On Sunday, June 25, 1950, the United Press dispatch began:

"The Russian-sponsored North Korean Communists invaded the American-supported Republic of South Korea today." Two years later, in the presidential campaign of 1952, Dwight D. Eisenhower promised, if elected, to go to Korea to seek an end to the conflict. Adlai Stevenson said in response: "The General has announced his intention to go to Korea. But the root of the Korean problem does not lie in Korea. It lies in Moscow."[1]

In retrospect, each of these events had its separate logic. The Czech takeover was the final step in the consolidation of the Soviet position in Eastern Europe. Earlier steps had not been seriously resisted. Some had been sanctioned in wartime agreements or in Churchill's wartime conversations with Stalin. Like Lenin in Russia, Mao in China moved into a vacuum — again the rotten door. He was then thought a Soviet instrument; this seems now an impossibly fantasy. That the North Koreans invaded South Korea is not in doubt; the subsequent efforts to portray it as a riposte to South Korean aggression proves only that, with enough faith, some will believe anything. But that the Soviets sponsored the action as part of the larger strategy of Communist expansion is very much in doubt. Far more likely, as with much since in that part of the world, it was an act of local initiative; were it to happen now, this would be believed. But together the effect of these events was devastating. Those who hoped for accommodation were silenced.

Henceforth the Cold War was the reality. Those who questioned were no longer defeated in argument. They were suppressed. Searching out the doubters became for some an industry and for Joseph McCarthy a career.

McCarthy, however, was a mindless aberration, soon to be struck down by alcohol and his inability to distinguish his friends from his enemies. The basic ideas of the period came from a far more reputable figure: John Foster Dulles. They were not doctrines of great sophistication or depth. Even at the time they were regarded by many with doubt. Dulles was never an object of instinctive popularity or trust. But ideas do not need to be deeply right to be deeply influential. Better that they fit the prevailing mood and need.

John Foster Dulles

Once war could be justified in its own terms — a brave participant sport with medals to the contestants and land and lesser spoils to the winner. This is no longer so. The justification must now be fully above economic interest. One cannot say that war is good for the Air Force, for the supplying industries or even that it sustains employment or output in the economy at large. As with war, so it was with mobilization of energies short of war – the Cold War. Even the defense of free enterprise against Communism by then raised questions. The passion for free enterprise was too obviously related to the revenues therefrom. And those who were most likely to suffer in its defense were those who were paid the least.

Defense of freedom was a much better case and one that was much used. But this was an argument with which those who most disliked the Soviet Union were not completely comfortable. Radicals defended Roosevelt, Mrs. Roosevelt, unions, a better distribution of wealth and the emerging welfare state in the name of freedom. Freedom could obviously be abused, be damaging. It was accepted in the early fifties that some had misused their freedom by espousing Communism, by holding pro-Communist thoughts or by being insufficiently passionate in their Americanism. By those who were most impressed with the Soviet menace this was deemed highly inimical. Freedom, clearly, was not an unqualified good. It was not, in consequence, the best case against Communism.

It was John Foster Dulles who came up with the completely acceptable doctrine on which to base the Cold War, one that avoided all embarrassment. The Cold War had nothing to do with economics; indeed, an excessive preoccupation with material values was a basic fault of the other side. Freedom was mentioned but was not central. The Cold War was a crusade for moral values — for good against bad, right against wrong, religion against atheism. It was the defense of the faith of the average, neighborly, God-fearing American — one's own beliefs and those of the people next door.

For this Dulles could turn to the faith of his fathers. He grew up with it in the small city of Watertown in far northern New York where his father was the Presbyterian minister. The countryside was a step away. As a boy Dulles sailed on the waters of Lake Ontario. His companion was his younger brother, Allen Welsh Dulles, his partner at law and in the Cold War battles to come.

From Watertown Foster went to Princeton and was intended by his parents for the ministry. However, early on he persuaded them he could do God's work almost as adequately were he a lawyer. So, after going as a young assistant to The Hague and Versailles Conferences and seeing the great in diplomatic discussion, he settled down to the practice of corporation law. By the age of thirty-eight, he was the senior partner of Sullivan & Cromwell, the most prestigious of the great Wall Street law firms. There he made his career.

This involved a certain wandering from his faith. Wall Street is not the epitome of church-going, small-town America. People do not think of corporation lawyers as being primarily concerned with God's work. They are believed, no doubt accurately, to have more remunerative clients. This was especially so of Dulles. In 1929, as I've earlier told, he was a director of the Shenandoah and Blue Ridge Corporations, the classic aberrations of that larcenous year. Hundreds of millions of dollars were lost. Governor Thomas E. Dewey who launched Dulles in politics, explained later that Dulles took a temporary leave of absence from religion during this period.

However, almost everything about John Foster Dulles remains a trifle ambiguous. Almost all historians, friendly or otherwise, speak of his brilliant mind. But Harold Macmillan, who saw much of him, was reminded of a statesman of whom it was said, ". . . his speech was slow, but it easily kept pace with his thought."[2] Most believed him paranoiac where Communism was involved. But others held that he got along well with the Russians, for he was what they expected a capitalist to be. In the Suez crisis of 1955 - 56, he lined up with the Soviets against the British, French and Israelis.

It is certain that Dulles had an instinct for command. There is a kind of person who, out of the very certainty of his purpose, right or wrong, both assumes leadership and is conceded leadership. No quality so assures public success. Douglas MacArthur was such a man. So was Charles de Gaulle. So, though with slightly less inner certainty, was Winston Churchill. So, we have seen, was Lenin. An old Scottish saying celebrates this leader: "Where MacCrimmon sits is the head of the table." To be a MacCrimmon is far better than to have brilliance of mind, eloquence of speech or charm of personality.

In the years following World War II, bored with the law and even with making money, Dulles prepared himself for command. He returned to religion and took an active part in the affairs of the

National Council of Churches. He resumed his earlier interest in foreign policy and helped negotiate the peace treaty with Japan. For a few months, by appointment, he was in the Senate but he was defeated when he sought election on his own. His power of command did not extend to the average voter. In 1953, Eisenhower made him Secretary of State. He came to office, and so did his moral sanction for the Cold War.

John Foster Dulles was not a very popular figure with liberals of my generation. Many of us agreed with the judgment of Reinhold Niebuhr, the liberal theologian, who said that "Mr. Dulles' moral universe makes everything quite clear, too clear . . . Self-righteousness is the inevitable fruit of simple moral judgments."[3] So it is only fair to let him speak for himself. This he did at his father's church in Watertown on October 11, 1953, nine months after he became Secretary of State. It is the clearest statement we have or would wish of the ideas underlying the Cold War:

The terrible things that are happening in some parts of the world are due to the fact that political and social practices have been separated from spiritual content.

That separation is almost total in the Soviet Communist world. There the rulers hold a materialistic creed which denies the existence of moral law. It denies that men are spiritual beings. It denies that there are any such things as eternal verities.

As a result the Soviet institutions treat human beings as primarily important from the standpoint of how much they can be made to produce for the glorification of the state. Labor is essentially slave labor, working to build up the military and material might of the state, so that those who rule can assert ever greater and more frightening power.

Such conditions repel us. But it is important to understand what causes those conditions. It is irreligion.[4]

He added:

But it is gross error to assume that material forces have a monopoly of dynamism. Moral forces too are mighty. Christians, to be sure, do not believe in invoking brute power to secure their ends. But that does not mean that they have no ends or that they have no means of getting there. Christians are not negative, supine people.

Jesus told the disciples to go out into all the world and to preach the gospel to all the nations. Any nation which bases its institutions on Christian principles cannot but be a dynamic nation.[5]

The Cold War was a moral crusade. It was also a religious crusade. And it came close to being a Christian crusade. There was more than a hint that a strong, even militant policy, so long as it avoided "brute power," would have the endorsement of Jesus.

There was a corollary here. Christians were as numerous east of the Iron Curtain as west. Their case, if religion was the issue, could not be less urgent than that of their coreligionists in Western Europe or the United States. Christians were as entitled to rescue as to defense. The Dulles case for the Cold War thus became a case for liberation, for rolling back the Iron Curtain. This Dulles at first proclaimed. However, in 1956, when the Hungarians rose in revolt, that promise was revoked.

Thus the setting. On the Soviet side was the proclaimed commitment to world revolution and a sequence of actions that could easily be interpreted as affirming it. In the West was the matching moral and religious commitment to liberation from Communism, or much language that could be so interpreted. The world was set for a dangerous passage.

The Cold War in Washington

The nineteen-fifties in Washington were the years not of Eisenhower but of Dulles. The idea of the irrepressible conflict went virtually unchallenged. The questioning to which, in a democratic society, every important action of the state should be subject was almost completely in

421

abeyance. I saw this, in a minor way, at first hand. I was cochairman with Dean Acheson in the latter fifties of one of the subsidiary organs of the Democratic Party, the Democratic Advisory Council. Acheson was chairman for foreign policy, I for domestic policy. The Council was, by common agreement, the most liberal wing of the opposition — the leading edge. At our meetings Acheson attacked Dulles lucidly, brilliantly and with resourceful invective for being too soft on the Soviets. The debate on his draft foreign policy resolutions consisted almost exclusively of efforts — by Adlai Stevenson, Averell Harriman, Herbert Lehman and other moderate members — to tone down his declarations of war. That was the opposition to Dulles.

At the more practical level, the Pentagon in these years developed weapons systems that were often duplicating or competitive and which were routinely approved. The word Pentagon itself now became a synonym for military bureaucracy and power, and a large and growing weapons industry responded to its will. Men moved with ease from managing the procurement of weapons in Washington to managing their development or manufacture in California. Few spoke against their decisions. The Armed Services Committees of the Congress endorsed all. In 1945, Robert Oppenheimer, the architect of the atomic bomb, was the most heroic figure in the history of American science. A reference to "Oppy" was the highest American achievement in the art of name-dropping, superior if anything to a British reference to Winston, though hardly as imaginative as a French allusion to Charles. In 1953, Oppenheimer's security clearance was lifted; he was excluded from all Washington deliberation and meditation. His substantive sin was in expressing doubts about the wisdom and desirability of the H-bomb. The Oppenheimer case showed as nothing else could have shown that no one in official position, however prestigious, had the right of dissent.

The questioning and dissent outside the government were equally unimpressive. The best scholars in the universities studied Cold War strategy. So with particular prestige did the new Think Tanks. To have spent a summer in the fifties at the Rand Corporation, the special intellectual instrument of the Air Force, established the position of an economics, mathematics or political science professor for all the coming year. A sociologist so favored might not even return to his university. The intelligence agencies were seen as central to all Cold War strategy, and the most central of all was the Central Intelligence Agency. In these years the CIA was a convocation of intellectuals to the point of being mildly suspect.

The License for Immorality

The controlling doctrines of the CIA, on which as a former ambassador I can speak with firsthand knowledge, involved an important modification of the Dulles conception of the Cold War. The CIA accepted that the Soviets were bent on world revolution. This involved a selective response to Soviet propaganda. When

Soviet leaders affirmed this goal, they were believed. When, as later happened, they spoke of peaceful coexistence, they were held to be dissembling.

In addition to ambitions in all non-Communist countries (which more than incidentally required that countering force be deployed in all countries), the Communists were brilliantly and relentlessly unscrupulous. This was in keeping with the Dulles doctrine of a battle between morality and immorality, right and wrong, with the Communists always immoral.

But here a problem arose, as often it does when action seeks the sanction of universal rules. Although the battle was between morality and immorality, you could not fight immorality and remain pure. Once it might have been imagined that Christian principles were a weapon of independent force. The CIA was more practical. So, to fight Communism, it was given a specific exemption from the Dulles ethic; its scholarly members were given a special license for immorality. They were then placed under the direction of Allen Dulles.

There was no danger that this juxtaposition to his brother's principles would cause Allen embarrassment. As noted, there was a difference of opinion on the speed and subtlety of John Foster Dulles's mind. Allen's mind presented no such problem.

Intellectuals, we have seen, yearn to prove that they can be tough-minded and very tough. So it was with those who manned the CIA. The license for immorality was greatly exploited and much enjoyed. Not many gave thought to a day when, the Cold War having abated however slightly, the license for immorality would be revoked and the Foster Dulles-Watertown morality restored with retroactive effect. This happened. For the former licensees it would be an unhappy time.*

*The reader has a right to ask whether on such matters an author writes from foresight or the wonderfully greater advantages of hindsight. Without claiming always to eschew the latter, I can say that, when I went to India in early 1961, I was profoundly impressed by the political unwisdom, adventurist tendency and amateurism of the CIA operations. And

Khrushchev

As always, we know much less about what went on in the Soviet Union. That Soviet policy in the postwar years was founded on the idea of irrepressible conflict is also certain. This would be plausible if only as a response but it was more than that. And that any such policy must build if not a military-industrial power, then a military-bureaucratic power can also be assumed. Some consequences of the same

---

I was even more impressed by the embarrassment the Ambassador of the United States would suffer when, as inevitably would happen, these operations were known. (All involved the participation of enough Indians to ensure that, one day, some or all of their cover would be blown.) Drawing on the support of President Kennedy and Lewis Jones of the State Department, a principled conservative who then presided over South Asian Affairs, and also on powers recently accorded an ambassador over his mission, I abolished all of the nonintelligence operations of the CIA in India. (They were not thereafter restored, or so I've been told.) In Washington a senior CIA official was so angry and distressed that he came to tears. In India the competent officers engaged in intelligence reporting — whose functions were known to the Indians — were, in the end, I always thought, relieved.

circumstances will be the same.

But in both the Soviet Union and the United States events were in train in the fifties which would change the perception of the conflict — which would cause it to be seen ever less as a conflict of systems, ever more as a manifestation of power, military, industrial and bureaucratic, within the two countries. I attribute prime importance to five influences. They were Khrushchev, Cuba, the Vietnam war, the increasingly sharp and visible divisions within the Communist world and the persistent unwillingness of the human mind to accept persuasion that is in conflict with evidence. All who exercise power find this latter obstinacy by far the most annoying tendency with which they have to contend.

After nearly thirty years of rule, Stalin died in 1953. Five years later Nikita Khrushchev emerged as his successor, and he held power for the next six. He was then suddenly and summarily discharged from office. By any calculation he was one of the decisive men of the midcentury. He had been, as he fully acknowledged, an undeviating supporter of Stalin. Had he been otherwise, he would not have kept well. The nearly inescapable instinct of any man so situated is to continue things as before. Such is the whole tendency of bureaucratic interest and inertia, the most powerful of influences in our time. Khrushchev, incredibly, committed himself to a reversal of Stalinist policies. And in this he had major success. He publicly condemned the Stalinist terror and greatly reduced the role of fear in the government of the Soviet Union. He enlarged perceptibly the scope for debate, liberalized appreciably the intellectual and cultural life of the country and proclaimed the obvious truth that, after an atomic exchange, little would distinguish the Communist ashes from the capitalist ashes. He recurred repeatedly to the resulting foreign policy theme that there must be peaceful coexistence with the non-Communist world. He traveled with obvious enjoyment to other countries to make his case.

Stalin, he once told Jawaharlal Nehru (who told me), had made the name of the

Soviet Union a stench in the nostrils of the civilized world. His task was to see that this was changed. The effort included two visits to the United States — unrequited pilgrimages which somewhat resembled later journeys of American presidents to Peking. In Moscow, with a certain genius for the opportunity, he engaged in impromptu debate with Richard Nixon. He seems to have sensed, if he did not fully know, that millions of Americans would believe that anyone who argued with Nixon could not be wholly wrong.

The defenders of the idea of irrepressible conflict did not give up easily. They warned solemnly against Khrushchev: a typical Communist trickster; an infinitely devious man; a very clever peasant. Khrushchev had promised that socialism would bury capitalism. Better be literal and believe that he meant The Bomb. There could be no reconciliation with a man who took off his shoes in public. There can be no doubt that Khrushchev's diplomacy, including his visits to the United States and the United Nations, was a major turning point in the Cold War.

It also, much later, provided a flash of insight into the way the Cold War was coming to be perceived on both sides. In 1971 and 1974, Khrushchev's memoirs were published. Although there were then questions as to their authenticity, that he was the ultimate source is not now seriously in doubt. In the United States and possibly also in the Soviet Union any writer with the talent and imagination to bring off the fraud would be writing more profitably on his own. Khrushchev tells of his visit in 1959 to President Eisenhower at his "dacha" at Camp David. In the course of informal conversation one evening, Eisenhower told him of the pressure from his generals for weapons expenditure. In the end, the intention of the Soviets being cited and the security of the United States being at risk, he found himself giving in. He asked Khrushchev if he had had similar experience. Khrushchev replied that he had. He was subject to similar pressure. He, however, talked back firmly to his generals. True, he added, they went on to say that if denied the requisite resources, the security of the

Soviet Union against the United States could not be guaranteed. And then he too gave in. Khrushchev, perhaps fortunately, was in power in Russia when Cuba came onto the stage.

Cuba

There are countries, which in consequence of size, location and, though more rarely, the wise belief of their people that nature did not intend them to be heroes, are meant for historical neglect. One of these is Cuba. Another is Vietnam. Both, in these years, had a decisive effect on the ideas with which we are here concerned.

Cuba's first impact was in the spring months of 1961. In the previous year there had been the inspired journey of Gary Powers across the Soviet Union as the nations were meeting for a summit at Paris. That the moment called for caution was well beyond the mental reach of Allen Dulles. Next came the Bay of Pigs. This too was conceived, planned and executed by the CIA. Members of the new Kennedy Administration had accepted and even admired the boldness of the enterprise. Presently it developed that not since Joshua's trumpets at Jericho had there been a military operation in which there was so little rational expectation of success. A helpless band of half-trained refugees was landed from some rusty freighters on a badly selected beach. A few ancient Cuban planes frightened off the ships that were to give them further support. The victims were soon rounded up. The Cuban masses, detesting Communism as did Americans, were expected to rise. Of this there was no sign.

At the United Nations Adlai Stevenson was allowed to identify the pilots of the attacking expedition who had landed at Florida after largely missing the Cuban air force as defectors from Castro. Any other American involvement was indignantly, even aggressively, denied. These untruths unraveled within hours. Nothing in the Cold War years was more striking than the incapacity of the scholarly personnel of the CIA for talented falsehood. Perhaps this was not surprising. They had been well brought up in good families, had gone to good schools and been hired on the basis of character and intelligence. So they were without experience in sustainable mendacity.

These untruths and their exposure were the most consequential single feature of the events at the Bay of Pigs. The unhappy flight of Gary Powers in 1960 had been first described as a badly navigated excursion to look at the weather. Sensing better than most the danger of falsehood in a moral crusade, President Eisenhower had moved quickly to affirm the truth. Now, closer to home, there was mendacity on a much larger scale. And the special license was here being used not against the Communists but against the American people and, as in the case of Stevenson, the American government. It was being used, in other words, against the same people to whom John Foster Dulles's moral crusade was designed to appeal — to whom, in an address to the National Council of Churches, he had said: "But I believe that we can still follow the good American tradition of openness, simplicity and morality in foreign policy."[6]

The contradiction between claim and practice was too great. Cynical men were not bothered but cynics were not the people for whom the Dulles ideas were meant. And while Foster Dulles was now dead, the man in charge of immorality was still his brother Allen. (In the aftermath of the Bay of Pigs he was sacked. So tactfully did the Establishment deal with its own in those days it is doubtful if he ever knew he was a failure.) It should surprise no one that, in later years, discussion of the immorality of the Soviet Union would give way to an extremely intense discussion and investigation of the immorality of the CIA. The problem with an appeal to moral values is that such values can be deeply held.

A Look into the Pit

A year and a half after the Bay of Pigs came the Cuban missile crisis. Cuba again. The effect of this was on the concept of the irrepressible conflict itself. Until then discussion of the conflict had been hypothetical, even academic in tone. Generals made speeches threatening the Communists with nuclear annihilation and calling for its calm acceptance by all patriotic Americans. The response was much as to sermons threatening or promising eternal punishment. The fear is in the sermon, not the prospect. Now for a few tense and terrible days the prospect was faced. People looked directly into the pit. There can be no doubt as to the result: thousands and perhaps millions began to wonder if there was not some slightly less heroic but substantially more pleasant alternative. Though it was little noticed at the time, after the missile crisis the generals ceased to make the speeches.

Something else became evident from this crisis, at least to the President of the United States. It was that men of little moral courage who get caught up in the decisions are afraid to resist the accepted view, however catastrophic it may be. So, paradoxically, out of cowardice, the fear of being in dissent or of seeming to be weak, they urge the most dangerous course. During the missile crisis these were the men who advocated an attack on the missile sites, what was called a surgical strike. No one could say *they* lacked guts, the charge of which they were most afraid. The men of independent courage — Adlai Stevenson, George Ball, Robert Kennedy — urged restraint. Coming back from India a few days after the end of the crisis, I went to the theater one evening with President and Mrs. Kennedy. During the intermission we went out by the curtain and sat on the stairs near the stage. This saved the President from the handshakers and the autograph hunters. "I didn't vote for you, Mr. President, but I certainly admire you." He told me, with much feeling, of the recklessness of the advice he had received during the crisis. The worst, he said, was from those who were afraid to be sensible.

Vietnam

The Cuban education was brief and deep. The education by Vietnam was prolonged and, in the end, decisive. In one fashion or another, all the assumptions of conflict as framed by Dulles were there eroded. Only as this is seen can the Vietnam war be understood as one of the great watersheds of modern history. It was an evil and bitter thing, out of which came much light.

A crusade for moral purpose requires a certain minimal moral tone on the part of those for whom the crusade is being mounted. Armies would not have been dispatched to the Holy Land for the redemption of either Sodom or Gomorrah. The saving of South Vietnam allied the United States with individuals whose moral posture few could defend. The gallery included corrupt and despotic politicians, corrupt and cowardly generals and a vast assortment of independent larcenists. Moral purpose was most strongly manifested by those in opposition to the government. Often, if not invariably, moral purpose in Vietnam brought people into such opposition. Meanwhile the country's common soldiers showed little disposition to die for the indefensible gains and privileges of others. It was a thought to which American warriors were not immune.

Twenty years earlier the same conflict between precept and practice had arisen in China. Chiang Kai-shek and his supporters had also been greatly lacking in moral tone. But in the absence of direct military involvement the contradiction had not been so serious. With President Diem, the Nhu family and the politicians that followed as in a revolving door, the impression of villainy was inescapable. Marx had held that capitalism becomes vulnerable at its most advanced stage. Vietnam, like China, proved almost precisely the reverse. Both countries showed that, as capitalism emerges from feudalism, it is characterized by an anarchic rapacity that the people of the advanced capitalist countries cannot understand.

In the end, the American people

reacted, caused a President to retire, placed great pressure on his successor when he showed signs of enlarging the war into Cambodia and Laos and brought the Vietnam conflict to an end. It was a remarkable demonstration of democratically expressed will. It flowed from the very sense of moral outrage that, for the opposite ends, John Foster Dulles had sought to arouse.

The Vietnam war destroyed the moral sanction of the war against Communism. Our allies were too immoral. It eliminated also another prop to the doctrine of irreconcilable conflict. This was the concept of Communism as a unified, centrally-directed world conspiracy. Dulles had spoken of atheistic Communism; Dean Rusk, his equally Cromwellian successor, spoke of monolithic Communism. China was a Soviet Manchukuo. All official references during his long and diligent term of office — from 1961 to 1969 — were to the Sino-Soviet bloc.

The conception of Communism as a united world transcending national differences and aspirations was vital. It was what made it seem a new and powerful force in the world. It could then plausibly be presented as many-faced, calculating and conspiratorial, relentlessly probing for weak spots in the armor of the non-Communist world. A Communist world divided along national lines and with conflicts within itself lost much of its power, much of its menace and much of its conspiratorial aspect. Some parts might be led to search for friends in the non-Communist world. Polemics and policies would have to be modified accordingly. The Cold War as a conflict between right and wrong had an appealing simplicity. With division in the Communist world there would be complicating degrees of wrong.

It became evident, as the Vietnam war progressed, that the Vietnamese Communists, however much they might be helped by the Soviets and the Chinese, were fighting very much on their own. And through the nineteen-sixties, evidence accumulated of conflict between the Soviets and the Chinese. Soviet assistance to China was suspended; Soviet technicians were withdrawn or expelled. There was talk of minor fighting along the frontier, fighting that could only be a manifestation of suspicion and hostility, for neither country could be imagined to set much store by the real estate at issue. In early 1972, while the Vietnam war continued, Richard Nixon responded to opportunity in a manner that should be a lesson to more principled men. He made a pilgrimage to Peking. This was followed in May of the same year by a trip to Moscow and the affirmation of the new policy of détente. (The English meaning of détente remained obscure; in 1976, President Ford announced that he was dropping the term but not the emphasis on peace.) At a minimum, the policy signified the end of the doctrine of irreconcilable conflict, of one side seeking the destruction of the other at whatever cost to itself. The justification of the strategic arms race could no longer be found in the old ideas. The arms race itself was now the trap.

The Symbiotic Trap

At Potsdam in 1945, Truman told Stalin about the successful tests and imminent use of the atomic bomb. Stalin, according to the contemporary accounts, reacted calmly; observers thought that he did not appreciate the significance of the news. Soviet scientists have since told that he phoned Moscow the same day to order all possible acceleration in the Soviet development of the same weapon.

The competition followed. Each side develops the weapons that make obsolete those currently in use or on order. In each country scientists, engineers, the armed services and the supporting industries join the effort and are rewarded by the task. An example, spectacular but not atypical, of this broad-spectrum collaboration was Project Nobska at Woods Hole on Cape Cod in Massachusetts in the summer of 1956. Naval officers, scientists and engineers from the defense industries gathered for ten weeks that summer to consider the military opportunities deriving from the recent successful tryouts

443

of the nuclear submarine. Edward Teller was there. So was Rear Admiral L. P. Ramage and Admiral Arleigh Burke. From IBM came James S. Crosby. The Associate Director of Nobska was Ivan Getting, Vice-President for Research of Raytheon Industries; the Director was Columbus Iselin, the head of the Woods Hole Oceanographic Institute. The entire enterprise was under the auspices not of the military but of the National Academy of Sciences.

From such a congregation something remarkable could surely be expected. Something remarkable came — a nuclear missile that could be fired from a submarine while underwater, out of sight and undetectable, to devastate a target up to three thousand miles away. This was Polaris.

Polaris, it later developed, countered a threat that the Soviets, at the time, were only contemplating. But this is unimportant. By the nature of the symbiotic trap, the Soviets would have led if they could. Had they been leading, this would have increased the urgency of the meeting at Woods Hole.

On few matters has the capacity of adults, presumptively sane, for the polemics of the schoolyard been more manifest than in the effort to justify this contest by ascribing blame. The Soviets are guilty; therefore the United States must respond. The imperialists are guilty; therefore the people of the Soviet Union will defend themselves. The debate is precisely on a parity with one between the squirrel and the wheel.

The Economic Consequences

It comes down to this: the armed services of the United States want to exist; to exist they must have weapons. The weapons firms want to exist and make money; to do this, they must produce weapons. The Soviets provide the justification for this existence. We justify the same institutions and the same process in the Soviet Union. It is no longer believed that conflict between the two powers is necessary or inevitable; all know that neither system could survive the conflict. We are reduced

445

to believing that the competition prevents the conflict.

The classical New England scenery at Woods Hole celebrates the highest technological achievement of the contest. To visualize its economic effects one should travel west to Tucson, Arizona, and there visit the Davies-Monthan Air Force Base. Here the economic effects stretch almost to the horizon. Davies-Monthan is the world's largest used-airplane lot.

Some of the aircraft on the Davies-Monthan lot will be sold. There are good bargains here for poor countries seeking a small place in the sun, wishing to emulate the destructive tendencies of the more advanced civilizations at low cost. And there are better ones — newer, faster, more complicated — for nations that have just struck it rich in oil. But most of the planes will never fly again; here on the range they are headed for the last roundup. No matter what the original cost, however wonderful the original performance, the paths through the wild blue yonder lead but to the junkyard.

There is agreement even in high military circles that the naked weapons competition cannot go on. Some will ask the hard question, what will take its place? What of the jobs it provides? What will replace the purchasing power it generates? John Maynard Keynes proposed that the British government put bundles of pound notes into disused coal pits and fill the pits up. This would create jobs. And much more employment would be created by men digging out the pounds, and much demand would then be generated by the spending of the notes. The idea was never taken up; instead, in the post-Keynesian world, weapons expenditures — the cycle of design, production, obsolescence, replacement — have served instead. I once called it military Keynesianism.

All candid economists concede the role of military expenditures in sustaining the modern economy. Some have held that expenditures for civilian purposes — health, housing, mass transport, lower taxes leading to more private consumption — would do as well. The transition would be rather easy.

This ignores the entrapment. And it ignores the economic power that sustains the trap and keeps it shut. Behind a new manned bomber is the military and industrial colossus we have been here examining. It is strong and resourceful in defending its interest, and we may assume that it is strong and resourceful in the Soviet Union too. Back of improved housing and cities there is no similar power as there is no similar competition. There is only, by comparison, a vacuum.

One should also observe that there is a problem of magnitudes. For the price of a smallish fleet of manned supersonic bombers, a modern mass transit system could be built in virtually every city large enough to have a serious bus line. What would be built then?

The Beginning of Change

The question is one for a later word. Yet it could be that the economics of the entrapment is changing. And the change, and opportunity for escape, could come more rapidly than most imagine.

In all the industrial countries hitherto-disadvantaged groups are releasing themselves from the convention that they were meant, for reasons of race, class or national origin, to have less. They are asserting their claim to enjoyments — leisure, good housing, vacations, education, more than minimal clothing, cultural activities — formerly considered the prerogatives of the affluent or the rich. Along with this, a point to be noted presently, have come the unimaginably large public costs of a highly urbanized existence.

Similar forces in slightly different form are at work in the Soviet Union. There serious inequity in consumption is even more difficult to defend. So is a standard of living too far below that of the nonsocialist world.

The result in all of the industrial countries, socialist and nonsocialist, is an unprecedented demand on economic resources. This manifests itself in the Western industrial countries in wage claims and resulting inflationary pressures. Military budgets are somewhat more closely examined now than in the days when the planes that are rotting at Davies-Monthan were ordered. That scrutiny will, we must hope, continue and with luck become more severe. In the Soviet Union the pressure of competing claims, by all outward evidence, is even stronger. Popularity there too accrues to those who can offer more civilian consumption.

So there is a chance that, with passing years, the economic question will not be what will take the place of military spending. Rather, it will be how military resources can be economized to make way for the other, more urgent claims of an increasingly classless consumption. The economic pressures will be for agreement on arms limitation, not against it.

That is at least a prospect. But it would be unwise for men of reason in either the United States or the Soviet Union — anyone, indeed, with a concern for survival — to await the day and acquiesce in the present entrapment. That entrapment had better be confronted directly, a need to which I will return.

9.
The Big Corporation

The institution that most changes our lives we least understand or, more correctly, seek most elaborately to misunderstand. That is the modern corporation. Week by week, month by month, year by year, it exercises a greater influence on our livelihood and the way we live than unions, universities, politicians, the government. There is a corporate myth which is carefully, assiduously propagated. And there is the reality. They bear little relation to each other. The modern corporation lives in suspension between fiction and truth.

The corporate myth is of a disciplined, energetic, dedicated but well-rewarded body of men serving under a dynamic leader. He reflects the interests of the owners at whose will he serves. His subordinates carry out his orders or transmit them on to the minions below. This is the organization. Its purpose, like that of all business firms large and small, is to make money by making things — to do well by doing good. It does best when it serves the public best. This is accomplished through the market, to which the corporation is wholly subordinate. What the consumer most wants, the market, in prices and sales, best rewards.

Since the corporation is wholly in the service of the consumer, it cannot be in the service of itself; being subject to the power of the public, it cannot have any significant power of its own. Generations of students have learned their economics from Paul A. Samuelson, an early Nobel Laureate in economics, the pre-eminent teacher of his time. His textbook puts the position with clarity and simplicity: "The consumer, so it is said, is the king . . . each is a voter who uses his money as votes to get the things done that he *wants* done."[1] Anyone subject to sovereign power can have no power of his own.

This is the myth. But Professor Samuelson is a sensible as well as distinguished man. So, like other economists, he reverts to the reality when he leaves the classroom. He recognizes that corporations greatly influence their markets — the prices they charge, the costs they pay — that in the real world, to use his words, they are "price-administering oligopolists."[2] Thus they manage prices to which the not-so-sovereign consumer responds. And the corporation also shapes the tastes of consumers to its products. No one can fail to be aware of this power. The advertising that does it dominates our vision and pre-empts our ears.

The modern corporation also exercises power in and by way of government. This too is agreed. Its payments to politicians and public officials are believed by no one except the recipients to be acts of philanthropy or affection. And less mentioned but more important is the naturally advantageous relationship between the modern corporation and the public bureaucracy — between those who build cars and those who build highways, between those who make fighter aircraft and those who guide the Air Force. Between the modern corporation and the modern state there is a deeply symbiotic relationship based on shared power and shared reward.

The myth that holds that the great corporation is the puppet of the market, the powerless servant of the consumer, is, in fact, one of the devices by which its power is perpetuated. Colonialism, we saw, was possible only because the myth of higher moral purpose regularly concealed the reality of lower economic interest. Similarly here. Were it part of our everyday education and comment that the corporation is an instrument for the exercise of power, that it belongs to the process by which we are governed, there would then be debate on how that power is used and how it might be made subordinate to the public will and need. This debate is avoided by propagating the myth that the power does not exist. It is especially useful that the young be so instructed. By pretending that power is not present, we greatly reduce the need to worry about its exercise.

But not completely, for we do not eliminate entirely the associated unease. We sense that our lives are shaped and that government is guided by the modern corporation. The myth disguises but it does not reassure. It leaves those who head large corporations unhappy in the knowledge that they are not loved, wondering why newspapermen, politicians and intellectuals do not share their sense of their own virtue. In the Age of Uncertainty the corporation is a major source of uncertainty. It leaves men wondering how and by whom and to what end they are ruled. One response to this uncertainty will be obvious. It is to look through the myth at the reality of the modern corporation.

The Esalen Institute

One begins with an Arcadian scene. The modern corporation has power. Men love the exercise of power. And in the

455

corporation power must be shared. All but the most elementary decisions require the information, specialized knowledge or experience of several or many people. It is a world, as Charles Addams has observed, where there are no great men, only great committees. Our instinct in the exercise of power is always to our own appreciation, our own view of what should be done. To adjust to the view of others, to accept their information and experience, requires a sensitivity and a restraint that many do not have.

This is the reason that executives go to Esalen on the California coast below Monterey; Esalen seeks to provide the sensitivity and the restraint that the organized exercise of power requires.

One thinks of the effort of married couples to achieve greater harmony and understanding. And rightly so, for in its intimacy of association corporate life is marriage with love but without sex. There is the same need to understand; to civilize; to perfect an association; above all, to persuade the individual that, at some point in the exercise of power, his purpose must be subordinated, without sense of defeat, to that of another.

Since 1965, major corporations — Standard Oil of California and Memorex, along with the State Department and Internal Revenue Service — have been sending their executives to Esalen for sensitivity training, meaning the sensitive exercise of power. On occasion, the results have been astonishing. One communicant at Esalen found himself rejecting the world of shared power and the world as well. He forever abandoned his three-piece business suit, changed to jeans, allowed his hair to grow and remained on as a gardener. How the rest were changed we do not know. The world of corporate power is a carefully protected one. Even social investigators do not intrude. The personal habits of potentates and politicians have always been the stuff of conversation, as they are of history. The psyche, home life, personal hygiene, even the sex habits of the great corporate executive have been little studied. But what Esalen says about the intensely interpersonal exercise of power in the modern corporation is very plain.

From this interpersonal exercise of power, the interaction and resulting purpose of the participants, comes the personality of the corporation. No two are exactly alike. No two exercise power to precisely the same ends. A corporation in which scientists and engineers interact — IBM, ICI, Xerox — will be very different from one which, like Revlon or Unilever, survives by its skill in mass persuasion or even public bamboozlement. Some corporations will measure success primarily by earnings, others by their growth. In yet others technical achievement is a partial measure of accomplishment. Some corporations use the language of service and public responsibility. If men speak often enough of their virtue, they may well persuade themselves to its practice. Others see their corporation as the continuing shadow of the hard-boiled, moneymaking capitalist. Let the Boy Scouts and the do-gooders worry about truth and the public good.

Because corporations differ, no single enterprise fully exemplifies corporate history and personality. All, when studied, revert, except in unguarded moments, to their myth. The exercise of power so central to corporate personality is at least partly concealed. So the solution here has been to synthesize — to draw from the realities of numerous corporations the history that best illustrates corporate development and the modern corporate personality. Our corporation will be Unified Global Enterprises — UGE. Since UGE exists but does not exist, there was no one to defend its myth. Everything having to do with UGE, inside and out, could be seen without censorship.

The Founder

James B. Glow came to Chicago from Greenock on the Clyde below Glasgow in 1871. He opened a butcher shop on the South Side and presently went on to curing hams and making sausage. Within the decade he had developed a sizable meat-packing business. It was a time when things went rapidly. Thereafter, in the words of the official history of the firm,

"James Ballantyne Glow never looked back." By the end of the century Glow Packing, along with Swift, Armour, Wilson and Cudahy, was one of the Big Five.

It was big with a difference. The Swifts and the Armours dominated Chicago society; their pork and beef underwrote the cultural life of the city. James Glow and his two sons paid attention only to their business and to their church. They knew many of their men by their first names; they watched over their families' lives. Their rules were firm and implacable. No single worker could board with a married employee. With husbands away on the night shift, that was temptation. All employees were visited regularly by the company social and religious adviser, who was paid a modest salary by the company itself. Glow Packing, as would now be said, was involved.

The Glows were also famous, even in Chicago, for the work they could extract from their men in the course of a standard seventy-two-hour week, twelve-hour day. However, again there were differences. No

Glow plant ever worked on the Sabbath. And along with their weekly pay, Glow employees received, all at no expense, Bible lessons and tracts warning against alcohol, tobacco, spendthrift living and immorality. During the great strikes of the eighteen-nineties, Chicago bosses were hanged in effigy. Reflecting the deep religious feeling in his plants, James B. Glow was several times burned at the stake.

In Chicago in those years, it was said, the meat packers found a use for every part of the pig but the squeal. The Glows did better; they found a use for ingredients that had never been near a carcass. Glow sausages were known to a generation of Americans as Glowworms. The company held that it was an affectionate nickname derived from their shape.

In defense of the Glows, it should be said that, at the time, the standards of the meat-packing industry were not high. During the Spanish-American War more soldiers were felled by the embalmed beef than by the Spanish bullets. There is no reason to believe that Glow products were greatly more lethal than the industry average. And no other company learned its lesson so well. Glow Packing never thereafter failed to stress quality in its advertising.

There was also a happy side to this history. The discovery that a wide range of inexpensive vegetable products, suitably disguised, processed and flavored, could be sold as canned meat and sausage was what launched Glow Packing on a path different from Swift, Armour and the rest. For presently it began to develop its own sources of vegetable oils, oatmeal, cornmeal, cottonseed meal, wheat bran and, it was said although never admitted, freshly milled sawdust. From these materials it was a simple step on to breakfast foods, including the famous Corn Husk and Flaked Barley lines, and thence on to canned dog food and biscuits, as well as to glue and adhesives, liver extracts, regenerative drugs and mineral laxatives.

In 1910, James B. Glow, Jr., well trained in the family traditions, took over from his father; in 1922, in a step of far greater significance than even he could have foreseen, he bought the trade name and syrup formula of Uni-Cola. To this he added, a few years later, the companion beverage, Uni-Up. Uni-Cola owed its popularity to its modestly addictive qualities — the syrup contained an operative infusion of cocaine. Eventually Glow dropped the drug. He was troubled both by his religious convictions and the threat of government regulation. Sales did not suffer as had been expected, and the action has often been cited by business philosophers to show the essential harmony between private interest and the public good. In 1929, the name of the company was changed to reflect the wide range of food products and the new importance of the soft drinks. It became Glow Food and Beverage, Inc. The stock, now widely held, was a marked favorite in the boom that summer.

In the Depression, despite what its annual reports always cited as "basic strengths," sales and earnings of the firm were hit by the general slump. And James Glow, Jr., now in his late sixties, was becoming as unapproachable and autocratic as his father had been before him. He suspected all subordinates of wanting a share in his power; he was deeply averse to unions and the New Deal policies of Franklin D. Roosevelt. A memorable photograph of the period shows him being carried from his offices rather than to submit to a National Labor Relations Board order requiring a union election in his Chicago plant. There was a long strike; in the end, union recognition had to be accorded. The company was said in the trade to be foundering. James Glow, Jr., came to be known, out of his hearing, as The Last Glow. Arthur Francis Glow, his nephew and only male heir, came briefly into the family firm in these years but soon returned to his art collection and his lifetime interest in Japanese erotic painting. A. F. Glow was always called The After Glow.

With World War II things were much better. Younger men took hold. Demand for the company products expanded. The United States Army marched on C and K rations from Glow Food and Beverage, this time without noticeable peristaltic effect. In a striking departure from its regular operations, the company undertook the management of a large shell-loading plant in downstate Illinois. The operation was eventually successful. After D-day, Glow, Inc. organized logistics support for the Quartermaster's food operations in the European Theater of Operations. There was a glimpse of larger horizons.

UGE Today

James Glow, Jr., was finally hospitalized in 1947; his resignation became inevitable following his attempt to have his personal chauffeur made President of the Company. He died the next year. Harold McBehan became President and Chief Executive Officer, and what has ever since been called the Era of McBehan began. Many phrases have been used to describe the McBehan business philosophy, most of them from McBehan's own speeches: a concept of sustained growth. Professionalized management by professional managers. A partnership with people. Profit with service. Technology in the service of national security. The nation's host. Nutrition for a free people. Constructive acquisitions for balanced diversification. All these mirrored the thinking of the new and dynamic team that McBehan had brought with him from the Pentagon and the Harvard Business School.

In 1955 came the final change of name; Glow Food and Beverage became Unified Global Enterprises — UGE. "The 'H' is silent," the company house organ proclaimed. By now the old exclusive tie with food and beverages was a thing of the past. UGE was big in pharmaceuticals, electronics, missile guidance systems, computer software, modular dwellings, along with its insurance company, UGEAIR and UGEHOTEL.

Harold McBehan left in 1969 to become Assistant Secretary of Defense for Procurement Planning under Richard Nixon. The loss to the company was regretted. But an opportunity for public service in the critical area of national and free-world defense could not easily be refused. And it was recognized, even if not mentioned, that UGE, as a major supplier of equipment and components, would not suffer from McBehan's presence in this key post. No one expected or wanted favoritism. But no one doubted the advantages of a better understanding, a close working relationship between industry and government.

By the time of McBehan's departure UGE was seventh on the *Fortune* list of the 500 largest American industrials. Its Annual Report for that year counted sales offices in sixty-two countries, substantial manufacturing operations in twenty-four. "Your management," the Report said proudly, "directs a closely articulated, internally reinforcing, inherently dynamic enterprise that responds well to the capabilities that are fundamental to modern managerial methodology and systems." In early 1969, the stock of UGE was at its all-time high; earnings, reflecting the favorable effects from the consolidation and subsequent revaluation of intercorporate holdings and other advanced accounting practices, had reflected their sixteenth straight annual gain. Accounting, it was being shown, was a creative art. (In subsequent years the methods of UGE's accountants came under increasingly close scrutiny from both the Securities and Exchange Commission and private analysts. They were shown to have contributed almost as effectively to earnings as the managerial techniques for which the company is justly celebrated.)

Not everything was good in these years. McBehan acquisitions had attracted the attention of the Department of Justice. The company was the subject of a suit calling for divestiture of its insurance affiliate and its advanced electronics subsidiary. Liberal economists and lawyers hailed the action as a landmark step in halting the trend toward increased industrial concentration. The issue was resolved after lengthy court action by a consent decree limiting further acquisition and providing for the divestiture of UGE's automobile rental business. The settlement, which attracted little attention, was worked out for UGE by a team of experienced antitrust lawyers, nearly all of whom had previous experience in the Department of Justice. Legal costs were substantial.

Command Post

Since 1965, more than a third of all UGE employees have been in overseas operations; by the late sixties approximately one half of consolidated earnings were from outside the United States. Brussels, the home of EEC, NATO and numerous satellite organizations, is the multinational capital of Europe. Streetwalkers and mendicants address their prospects as Your Excellency. UGE, somewhat exceptionally, operates from Paris. "The intellectual, artistic and quality consumer goods capital of Europe," Harold McBehan said in his speech at the opening of the new headquarters at La Défense. Also, better food, better whores and the Crazy Horse Saloon, a jovial and somewhat alcoholic minor executive was heard to add. There were more substantial reasons, although they were little publicized. UGE has always enjoyed close and mutually beneficial relationships with French political and military leaders. The Paris location was not unrelated to promised tax advantages and anticipated military orders.

Since 1962, the world headquarters of UGE has been not Chicago but New York. The dominent theme of every age is reflected in the grandest of its structures — religion in the cathedrals, the nation state in Versailles, the Industrial Revolution in the railroad depots, modern sport in the Astrodome and its counterparts, the modern corporation in the skyscrapers. The UGE tower dwarfs the lesser structures across Sixth Avenue at Rockefeller Center. Critics described it as "gross, pretentious, in its own way hideous." Harold McBehan is not known to have heard. "This building," he said at the opening, "is our signature. It writes three letters large in the heavens — UGE."

The board of directors meet in the boardroom on the 79th floor — "the command post." Harold McBehan has called it the great room. The board of directors is the voice of the stockholders, the men and women who own the corporation. From their lips come the marching orders; they are the ultimate authority.

That is the myth. When the first James Glow died, a large chunk of stock went to his three daughters. None of this is now in the family. More went into the Glow Foundation which James B. Glow, Jr., and his brother established for the propagation of the essential principles of free enterprise, a philanthropy which also reduced substantially the impact of the inheritance tax. In subsequent diversification moves by the Foundation much of this stock was sold. Arthur Francis Glow — The After Glow — sold some of his stock when he established his gallery; more went for his Institute for Oriental Erotic Art, yet more to his four former wives in alimony. All of McBehan's acquisitions involved new issues and an exchange of these for the stock of the company being acquired. UGE stock holdings were thus further dispersed.

In 1932, the two noted Columbia University professors, Adolf A. Berle and Gardiner C. Means, studied the control of the two hundred largest nonfinancial corporations in the United States. Nearly half, they discovered, were controlled by their management. No power remained with the owners to hire or fire the managers; the management appointed the directors who represented the stockholders. The directors did not appoint the managers. There would now be no question as to UGE's membership on the management-controlled list. No individual stockholder owns as much as one percent of the stock of UGE. None of the directors owns more than the requisite qualifying shares. All the directors were selected by Harold McBehan and were voted in automatically by proxies returned for the management slate. McBehan's tests for selection were high standing in the financial world, past political service in Washington and a reputation for never interfering with management decisions. The average age of the directors was, until recently, sixty-seven. This has now been lowered slightly by the addition of a black, a consumer advocate and a nun. With the others they meet for two hours every two months and ratify decisions that have already been taken and which several of the board members do not understand. Two cannot remain awake. None has ever opposed management on any matter of more than cosmetic importance. All recognize the overwhelming advantage of those whose information is derived from day-to-day involvement with planning and operations. If UGE were losing money or moving into bankruptcy, the directors, prodded by the two bankers on the board, might well be led to question the quality of the management. Nothing short of this, or the suspicion of major fraud, would cause them to act. The board has confidence, on the whole justified, in the honesty of UGE's management.

The Washington Scene

The Washington office of UGE is on H Street. It is modest as compared with those in New York and Paris but by no means obscure. What is called the UGE presence in Washington is considered vital for company welfare. Tax legislation and decisions; food labeling and truth in advertising; drug safety; product safety and standards; environmental impact statements; Pentagon orders and intentions; intelligence filtering in from countries where UGE does business; all of these and a dozen other matters call for the constant vigilance of the UGE Washington men. For particularly sensitive operations against the public interest, they engage the services of two large Washington law firms famous for their public-spirited assistance to worthy public causes. Neither Harold McBehan nor any other UGE man has ever overthrown a foreign government or would know how to begin. Their men do play a large part in the government of the United States; otherwise the Washington office would not be worthwhile. UGE has come far since James B. Glow, Jr., traveled each year to the Capitol to lobby against imports of Argentine beef. The UGE Washington men govern without being known, without having had the risk or expense of running for office. It is this public role more than any other which makes UGE a source of unease and uncertainty.

The Technostructure

When he went to the Pentagon, Harold McBehan was succeeded by Howard J. Small, previously Executive Vice-President for Corporate Operations. Howie, as he is known in the firm, is in the same salary bracket as was McBehan — $812,000 a year plus deferred compensation and pension rights. He is entitled also to stock options but since the recent slide in the value of the stock, these have not been mentioned. Howie's jet carries as large and attentive an entourage as any sovereign's. But Howie, unlike McBehan, is little known outside the firm. He is a two-pack-a-day smoker, drinks to keep going, and, were he a vital factor in the enterprise, his heart condition would be the source of the gravest concern. The Dow-Jones wide tape would carry his electrocardiogram and also his latest lung X-ray. In fact, no investor gives Howard J. Small's health the slightest thought. McBehan's departure completed a process long under way, the passage of power in UGE from individuals to organization. Howie doesn't matter.

Again the myth and the reality. The myth of modern company management is of a hierarchy in which orders flow down from above. The reality is of a circle. At the center of the circle is the top management — in the case of UGE, Howard J. Small and his staff of executive vice-presidents, financial vice-presidents, vice-presidents, assistant vice-presidents, the controllers, the treasurer, the counsel, the head of the Washington office. In the next circle are the heads of the companies at home and abroad that make up what is still called the UGE family. In the ring beyond are those whose specialized knowledge contributes to decisions in the many constituent companies and divisions — the engineers, scientists, sales managers, advertising specialists, dealer relations men, designers, lawyers, accountants, economists, the men who manage the computers. Next beyond are secretaries, clerks, typists — the white-collar workers. Next are the men who supervise production on the floor, get out the goods. In the final outer ring are the blue-collar workers.

In the inner rings of UGE there is the

power that proceeds from position. In the middle rings there is the power that proceeds from knowledge. In the outer rings the power proceeds from numbers and union organization. Power flows in as well as out. Corporate action is the product of an intense interaction between the rings. Reward — higher pay, more power — goes to the man who enlarges his space on one or another of the rings. This he can do by coming up with a product, a label, a slogan, a commercial or a campaign that increases sales. That is why UGE emphasizes growth as a goal; a great many people in UGE are rewarded in pay, power and perquisites when there is growth on their own turf. With so many working for growth, UGE grows, and growth is its test of success. Economists and politicians speak often of the social gains of economic growth. These they often believe to be an abstract good unrelated to pecuniary interest. Growth is also very good for UGE. This may have even more to do with the emphasis it receives.

The Practice: Eindhoven

UGE is an American company but the corporation is worldwide. The corporation's most notable achievement is to diminish national traits and make all industrial countries alike. Americans are blamed for this. In fact, it is a powerful tendency of the corporation, whatever its national origin. For large tasks the socialist countries too use the corporation — an inevitable convergence.

We see this in Eindhoven, a city of 190,000 people, a couple of hours' drive south and east of Amsterdam. Once it had its moment in world history; in 1944, it was taken by Montgomery's armies when the further jump to Arnhem proved a bridge too far. Since 1891, Eindhoven has been the headquarters of Philips Gloeilampenfabrieken, which in 1974 was ranked third in size among the industrial corporations outside the United States by *Fortune* and thirteenth in the world. This came from sales that year of electrical goods and other technical hardware of $9.5 billion and employment, in some sixty countries, of 412,000 people.

The Glows have long since gone from UGE, and nobody weeps. In the more durable Dutch tradition there is still a Philips on the Philips board. James Glow's concern for the chastity of his workers and their wives is remembered around Chicago only as a minor manifestation of a dirty mind. Howie Small's mind turns to his working force only when they want a wage increase or threaten a strike. He then calls for a firm stand on principle by those responsible and later accepts a compromise. In Eindhoven the Philips presence is still a powerful thing; workers and the firm still live in close association with each other. There are only two ways, it is said in Eindhoven, to be fired from Philips — to shoot the chairman of the company or to molest the coffee girl. The first is recommended, for the second is more serious.

But in Eindhoven, too, the trend is the same. Once the company housed its workers, saw to their health, was concerned with their education. Those tasks have now gone or are going to the city or state. Once the company instructed the workers as to its wishes. Now it asks the union. In talking of the power of the modern corporation, an important distinction must be made. Its public power increases. Its parental power steadily diminishes.

Philips, like UGE, is a creature of its technostructure. In this respect, too, all corporations are alike. Whether in Eindhoven, New York or Houston the quality of the corporate performance depends not on individual brilliance but on organizational competence — on the success in choosing and combining the efforts of the men, and the rare woman, who fill the rings.

These men of the technostructure are the new and universal priesthood. Their religion is business success; their test of virtue is growth and profit. Their bible is the computer printout; their communion bench is the committee room. The sales force carries their message to the world, and a message is what it is often called. Alcohol is under interdict as an intoxicant but allowed as an adjunct of communion and as an instrument of friendly persuasion. Recreation is for regeneration of the business spirit, for a widened range of business contacts. Sex is for better sleep. The Jesuits of this austere faith are the graduates of the Harvard Business School.

The Harvard men were the first in the faith. They still are but now there are numerous subordinate orders. One of these trains at a French business school — INSEAD in the Forest of Fontainebleau. The technostructure of the corporation is a design for drawing on the specialized knowledge of different disciplines. In keeping with this, engineers work here with accountants, economists with marketing men. All and more make up what, needless to say, is called a team. From this comes experience of group effort. The word effort deserves emphasis. Neither here nor elsewhere does the business seminary favor the deeply reverenced leisure of the liberal university, the leisure that is assumed to rest and refresh the brain but which also serves excellently as an excuse for pleasurable idleness. In the corporation faith, the most important word is work.

There is little time for speculative theory. Learning is problem-solving. Following the technique pioneered at Harvard, instruction is by the case method, by practice in making the decisions that students hope they will soon be encountering in the executive suite.

The result of Harvard, INSEAD and the rest, still surprisingly unnoticed, is a race of men who, no less than the corporations they serve, are the same. National identity has been excised. They are not Dutch, not French, not English, not Belgian but all slightly American. Their first loyalty is to Philips, IBM, Exxon, BP, Nestlé; not to the Netherlands, the United States, Britain or Switzerland. Their uniform in all countries, the occasional eccentric apart, is the same: a quiet suit, a careful tie, decently polished shoes. The best of them can be dropped on a week's notice into Brussels, Geneva or Indianapolis. There, like a coin in a slot, they will immediately produce. The proletarian, Marx avowed, knows no motherland. This has never been quite true. But it is true of his present-day employer, the modern corporate man.

The Corporate World

Harold McBehan coordinated the worldwide operations of what, in one of his more thoughtful moments, he called his empire by airplane. Overseas managers were summoned once a month to La Défense. The heads of the U.S. operating divisions met monthly in New York or in December at the company's depressing hotel and golf club in the Bahamas. The head of each division had a sales and profit goal for the year; at the meetings each explained how, given proper budget support by the head office, a decent break on consumer confidence and some accounting adjustments, the goals would be substantially exceeded.

Howard Small is also often airborne. But now the management team keeps itself current on all operations. The computer printouts are on Howie's desk every morning. Regularly he ratifies actions which he does not understand. They have been, he knows, well staffed-out.

Philips is less centralized. It likes to think of itself not as a corporation but as a federation. The heads of its over sixty national organizations are appointed by Eindhoven; major capital outlays are approved there. Then each of the national companies — some that manufacture and sell, some that only sell — are left to do their best. They are encouraged to become part of the local scene. In every country the Philips sign in neon lights is, indeed, an inescapable feature of the landscape.

Once every twelve months the heads of the national companies come together to report on operations of the past year and on plans for the next five. They assemble in Ouchy, not far from Lausanne in Switzerland — again the conscious denationalization. Not only do corporations plan; they have five-year plans.

There is a further, more important line of command. In Eindhoven and elsewhere in the Netherlands are some thirteen divisions (with one in Italy) concerned with the development and marketing of

Philips products — lamps, television sets, radios, appliances, heavy electrical apparatus and the rest. These product divisions deal directly with those who are making or selling their item in the national companies. A board of management keeps their work under review. Engineering, quality control and marketing virtuosity can thus be kept up to the same standard for the whole enterprise. Principals from different countries concerned with a particular line of products meet from time to time. There are scheduled company flights, and a fleet of airplanes stands by at Eindhoven to facilitate this travel. The Philips style is more staid than UGE but it hasn't eliminated executive movement.

Why Is It Unloved?

Why does UGE — or Philips — arouse unease? Why do they contribute so remarkably to the Age of Uncertainty? The things UGE makes are better, safer and, relative to the incomes of the buyers, much cheaper than the adulterated, indigestible and sometimes lethal merchandise of the ineffable Glows. No modern worker would remain for a day in the factory of the saintly James B. Glow. None would tolerate even for a day Glow's intrusive and prurient interest in his religious, alcoholic and sexual preoccupations.

Harold McBehan was a driven man; so is Howie Small. A philosopher from another time or world would marvel at their view of life; wonder why they so sacrifice their time and health; be puzzled by their curious concept of reward — the trivial obeisance of subordinates and money they do not have time to spend. He would wonder why they work so hard. He might think them foolish; he would not think them wicked.

From our view of UGE — and Philips — we can see how great is the conflict between myth and reality in the modern corporation and how this generates unease and suspicion. Where the myth departs so sharply from the reality, it is only natural to suppose that its purpose is to conceal. No one can believe that UGE is the powerless and passive instrument of market forces. No one with the slightest knowledge of UGE's Washington operations can believe that it is without power in the state. No one can believe that its management is the responsive servant of directors and stockholders. Yet all these things the myth affirms. Where so much must be done to conceal power, only one conclusion is possible. The exercise of power must surely be malign.

Some of the unease disappears when the corporation is looked at candidly and without the covering myth. UGE, when so examined, does not appear as a convocation of saints. Some of its achievements, in a rational world, would seem at least mildly insane. But much of its effort, and some of its exercise of power, is for the manufacture and sale of routine, useful and useless things. Thus does the unease diminish when the myth is dissolved. There remain the multinational operations of the corporation, which are regarded with special alarm. And also its relation to governments and the part it plays in the weapons culture.

The Multinational Syndrome

For the modern great corporation no place is too far away. It's as much in evidence in Hong Kong and Singapore as in New York, Brussels or Madrid. Howie Small's people have recently won a soft drink concession in the Soviet Union. It is intended to cut into the consumption of vodka. They have hopes for business in North Korea. Because it is everywhere, omnipresent and seemingly omnipotent, the multinational corporation is greatly celebrated in our time. On occasions of introspective ceremony the executives of multinational corporations themselves listen to grave lectures from American professors on how they transcend national power and undermine national identity. All who impart such wisdom, without exception, view the multinational corporation with grave concern.

Again we can be a trifle skeptical; were the multinationals as pernicious as their billing, we should hardly have survived until now. In no place does one see the multinational presence so vividly as in the tiny city-state of Singapore. The great international corporations bring in the materials, bring in the fuel, finance the production, make the products, house and feed those who come to buy or sell and take the products away to market. No one can be in doubt as to the result; they have remade the city in the image of the industrial West.

But one must ask if this is so bad. Once it was the pride of Singapore that it was a Little England — a small tropical port that had tennis, cricket, billiards, Scotch, *The Illustrated London News,* Dickens, all the benefits of British civilization. The impact of Philips and Chase Manhattan is different but who can say it is worse.

It is held that the multinational corporation comes in from abroad to influence the decisions of national governments. In consequence, Frenchmen or Canadians are governed, in some measure, by foreign corporations. This is so. But domestic corporations seek, as does UGE, to persuade or even instruct the government of the countries that gave them birth. This is the basic tendency of the large corporation, national or international. It could be that the foreign corporation, conscious of its external origins, proceeds with more tact than does the large domestic firm. UGE can be thrown out of Canada as Canadian Pacific could not. The fact of life in all industrial countries is corporate power, not international corporate power.

Finally, one must ask if the suppression of national identity is to be deplored. The assertion of such identity by Frenchmen, Germans and the British in the first half of this century brought millions of people to their death in two intra-European wars. In the general view the European Common Market came into existence as the result of a sudden access of economic enlightenment after World War II. Miraculously, after two hundred years, statesmen sat down and began reading Adam Smith on the advantages of the division of labor and how production was limited only by the size of the market. More plausibly, the EEC came into being because, for the modern multinational corporation, national boundaries and the associated tariffs and trade restrictions were a nuisance. It had a better way of keeping foreign competition under control. That was to be the competitor.

What Comes After General Motors

The large corporation is here to stay. Those who would break it up and confine its operations within national boundaries are at war with history and circumstance. People want large tasks performed — oil recovered from the North Sea, automobiles made by the million to use it. Large tasks require large organizations. That is how it is.

Nor can the individual decisions of corporations be too extensively second-guessed. There can and must be rules; but within the rules there must be freedom to decide. More than an individual, an organization, if it is to develop and be effective, must have autonomy and ability to act. The one thing worse than a wicked corporation is an incompetent one. The one thing as bad as a wrong decision is a decision that is greatly delayed.

The ultimate answer for the multinational corporation is multinational authority — government that is coordinate in scope with the corporations being regulated. The decline in national identity is paving the way for this solution. There is no danger, however, that it will come too soon. In Europe international authority is distantly in sight. Elsewhere it is not.

Meanwhile for national governments and national corporations the only answer is a strong framework of rules that align the exercise of corporate power with the public purpose. This is not an exercise in hope and prayer. It is one of the dominant trends of the times. What a corporation can do to air, water, landscape, truth and the health and safety of its customers and the public is far more carefully specified than it was a mere decade ago. Ralph Nader didn't bring this regulation. The need brought Nader. It will continue.

Of further reforms there is less discussion. Especially in the United States it is an article of the free-enterprise faith that General Motors — and UGE — are the final work of God and man. Other things can be perfected; these cannot. A divine hand guided the corporate building by the churchly Glows, by the profane and secular McBehan and even by Howie Small. The result is perfect. To suggest the possibility or need for further change is the modern heresy.

Still, there are suggestions. Putting representatives of labor, minorities, women and the public on boards of directors is discussed. The participation of trade unions is very much an issue in Europe. It seems to me, on balance, a dubious reform. Those members of the board of directors who do not participate in day-to-day management are, we have seen, without power. So accordingly will be the representatives of labor, consumers and the public who are added by this change.

A better line of development would be to abolish boards of directors in the large firms now that they have no function. These would then be replaced with a board of public auditors, which would keep out of management decisions but ensure the enforcement of public laws and regulations, report on matters of public interest, otherwise keep management honest and ratify or, in the event of inadequacy or failure, order changes in the top management command.

You will ask who then would represent the stockholder. The answer is that no one does now. The shareholder in the modern large corporation is without power and without function. He (or she) is also obsolete. A further plausible development would be to pay off such functionless stockholders in bonds and have the dividends and capital gains accrue to the public. That, all will say, is socialism. It is so. But it is socialism after the fact. The great corporation, as it develops, takes power away from the owners, from the capitalists. The most profound tendency of the modern corporation, one that is rarely mentioned, is to socialize itself.

It socializes itself in two ways. It takes all power from its owners — disenfranchises the capitalists. It also makes itself socially indispensable. We now know that if a corporation is large enough, it can no longer be allowed to fail and go out of business. The recent history of Lockheed, Rolls-Royce, Penn Central, the other eastern railroads in the United States, Krupp, British Leyland, British Chrysler affirms the point. All have been rescued or are supported by government. Modern socialism is not the work of politicians or college professors. It is the accomplishment of corporation executives and those to whom they owe money. They are the cutting edge. They are the men who appear in Washington or Whitehall on the day when bankruptcy seems inevitable to ask the government to come in.

On this too Howard Small — Howie of UGE — has shown the way. In line of duty Howie makes frequent speeches to groups of concerned citizens. It is something he must do. The speeches are written for him by a Yaleman who was once an Associate Editor of *Time*. They dwell on the tradition of rugged independence in American life; the dangers of big government; the withering effect of welfare on the morale of those receiving it; and they do not fail to mention the omnipresent threat of socialism. This is the way Howie Small put it in his speech to his own stockholders only last year:

I speak to you now not as a businessman, not as your president but as an American — a deeply concerned American. My message is government —the ever-expanding maze of government regulations, the ever-increasing cost of bureaucracy, the dead hand of government on enterprise, the blighting impact of welfare checks on people, what the handout state is doing to the work ethic, the belief that all problems can be solved by throwing a little of your and my money at them. In a word, I speak to you of socialism — socialism not as some distant threat but socialism here and now.

My friends, the time has come when we must reverse this deadly trend — when you must work to do it; when I must work to do it; when together we must put our shoulders to the wheel and stand firm against the tide.

Later in his speech Howie called for "an adequate national defense" and spoke of other areas "for constructive cooperation between government and industry." He said:

I am proud to announce such a step today. In keeping with the rest of the airline industry, UGEAIR has been caught between ever-rising cost and stable passenger revenues, problems, I need not tell you, that are not of our own making. As you have read, we proposed a government takeover of the line. Instead, in a constructive step, Washington has promised an increase in the airmail subsidy, an equally constructive support to our short-term debt refinancing and a constructive guarantee of our new equipment financing. This is the kind of constructive association between industry and government which we should welcome in a free society. It is our best guarantee against the march of socialism.

Howie Small is thus strongly opposed to socialism. But, though he does not know it, he makes a distinction between socialism for the profitable firm and socialism for the failing corporation. There is a somewhat similar distinction between socialism for the rich and socialism for the poor.

We are not through with the corporation. What has just been said assumes that it can be made subordinate to the state and that it can thus be made subject to the public interest. But the corporation is powerful in the state — in the very public institution by which it must be controlled. Surely there is a contradiction here. How can the corporation be controlled by the institution it controls? Surely one must inquire if the corporation is not, in fact, an extension of the modern state — an integral part of larger arrangements by which we are governed. To this thought, and to its particular application to the issues of peace and war, we shall return.

10.
Land and People

We have been talking mostly of the few countries, capitalist or socialist, that as the world measures such matters are exceedingly rich. However serious their other problems, they have gone far to solve the one that for most of the people of the world is transcendent. That is poverty — poverty so severe that it faces those afflicted with the stark problem of how to keep on living. Whether or not they will succeed is for most of the world's people still the greatest uncertainty of all. To the ideas that explain poverty we now turn.

Of these there are an abundance. There is no economic question so important as why so many people are so poor. There is none concerning the human condition to which so many different and conflicting answers are given with so much confidence and such nonchalance. The people are naturally lacking in energy and ambition. Their race or religion makes them so. The country is wanting in natural resources. The economic system — capitalism, socialism, Communism — is wrong. There is insufficient saving and investment. Property, profit or the rewards of toil are not secure. Education is inadequate. There is a shortage of technical, scientific or administrative talent. There is a legacy of colonial exploitation, racial discrimination, national humiliation. Every day in every part of the world every one of these explanations is offered. For mankind's most common affliction we have a multitude of diagnoses, each offered with the utmost casualness. Poverty is a painful thing. It would be well if we knew the cause.

There is no one answer — obviously. It is because so many explanations have a little truth that so many are offered. But one cause of poverty is pervasive. That is the relationship, past or present, between land and people. Understand that, and we understand the most general single cause of deprivation.

The reason is simple. Everything that allows of the first escape from privation — food, clothing, elementary shelter — comes from the land. If these cannot be provided, there is poverty. If they cannot be increased in relation to the numbers of the people, it endures.

In India, Bangladesh, the Nile Valley, Indonesia, the people who work the land are exceedingly numerous. Their product, no matter how divided, provides only the merest subsistence, or less. That improved culture — fertilizer, more water, high-yielding hybrid cereals, better cultivation, better plant protection — could increase yields is not in doubt. The increase can be dramatic; the Green Revolution is real. But these cost money. If all that is produced must be consumed to live, there will be nothing left over to invest in fertilization, irrigation or better seed stock. Also there will be nothing left over, and no incentive to invest, in any case, if all of the product above a bare minimum goes to a landlord or in taxes. And there will be no incentive to invest and improve unless there is education in the advantages of the new methods and the required techniques. For some calculations one does not need a professional economist.

But this is not all. Perhaps a benign Providence or, often more improbably, a wise, efficient and benign government aided by oil or the World Bank will provide some of the means for agricultural improvement — the canals, fertilizer, seed and the guidance in their use. And perhaps land reform will give land to the cultivator. In India these things have partly happened. Indian foodgrain production averaged 63 million metric tons annually in the nineteen-fifties. So far in the nineteen-seventies (which have included some very bad years) it has been 104 million metric tons.[1] But when production increases, the ghost of the Reverend Thomas Robert Malthus then walks. The increased food is consumed by the increased population. There is an equilibrium of poverty; when broken, it re-establishes itself. That too is the history of modern India. In 1951, there were 361 million Indians. In 1976, to eat the added food, there are an estimated 600 million. A revolution, it has often been said, devours its children. Green revolutions are different; they devour themselves. We shall know much about poverty if we know the answer to two questions: How does the equilibrium of poverty develop? How can it be broken?

The Punjab

It has, in fact, been broken on one part of the Indian subcontinent. To the outsider the vast population of this area — India, Pakistan, Bangladesh — however diverse in religion, culture and language and however contentious within itself, has always seemed completely homogeneous in its poverty. But those close to the scene have long remarked on a region of substantial and increasing well-being. This is the Punjab, the great plain that stretches across northern India and Pakistan. Here the fortunes of history and development have given the average farmer a sizable plot of land. Farms of fifteen to thirty acres, vast by Indian or Pakistani standards, are commonplace. To this land comes water from the five great rivers that give the Punjab its name. The result, including the land along the Indus to the south, is, incomparably, the world's greatest irrigation project. And the farms that do not draw on the canals have tube wells that tap the vast underground lake which lies below the plain — a lake that until recently threatened to rise as a result of leakage from the irrigation canals, bring up salt and reduce to infertile marsh the cropland on the surface and which, in an agreeable symbiosis, the tube wells now help to keep under control.

The effect of irrigation is to give the family more land in a smaller area. It allows, as well, of the more effective use of fertilizer, which is also a substitute for land. And with water and fertilizer there is an improved response from hybrid grains. From the increased product comes the wherewithal to buy the fertilizer and improved seed and even, on occasion, a tractor. Improvement then continues. There is an incentive to protect the gains, partly by family limitation, partly because well-prepared sons and daughters move readily into urban occupations. It is the Indian Punjab, predictably, that has first moved toward making family planning not permissive but compulsory. It is from the Indian Punjab that much of the increased production of grain which I mentioned a moment ago has come.

So the equilibrium can be broken. Perhaps, as people elsewhere in Pakistan and India believe, the Punjabis work harder than the rest. But this also is made possible by better food. Perhaps, by nature, they are technologically more apt and progressive. This too is widely believed. It could be because their higher income has long sustained better schools. And their more sophisticated farming provides an early acquaintance with machinery and other technology. What is not in doubt is that the good fortune of the Punjabis in India and Pakistan begins in a better relationship of land and people.

The Possibilities

There are, in principle, four ways in which the equilibrium of poverty can be broken. One is to provide more land or its effective substitute in the form of water and fertilizer. For this the cultivator must, as in the Punjab, have a sufficient minimum of land with which to start.

The second possibility is to alter land tenure to reward the efforts of the people with what they produce. For this too there must be enough land.

The third answer is for people to breed less. The fourth is for them to disappear. If land supply is indeed insufficient, only these last two answers will serve.

Birth Control

The control of population always seems the wonderfully obvious solution. It is practiced with ease by the affluent to protect their well-being. For the poor, unhappily, the population increase is part of the equilibrium of poverty. People of means *have* a standard of living to protect. The poor — a highly indisputable fact — have not. The affluent get knowledge of contraceptives and the ability to pay for them as an aspect of affluence. The poor do not. Well-to-do people have a diversity of recreation. The poor, a point that religion and romantic fiction unite in ignoring, rely for much more of their limited recreation on sexual intercourse. It is the only moment of brightness and escape to which the worker from the fields returns. It is one of the very few enjoyments on which wealth is not thought greatly to improve.

Because the task is so unrewarding, governments have usually put their most congenitally inadequate minister in charge of family planning. Rats and locusts are controlled and epidemics are prevented by officials who measure their success by results. Births are controlled by people who measure success by the number and eloquence of their speeches and the weight of the pamphlets they distribute.

Many in the poor countries believe that the rich nations urge birth control because it is a painless way of being rid of them, and the remedy becomes even more attractive if the poor are dark, yellow or black. One consequence is a sensitive reluctance by many in the affluent countries to press the case for birth control. This is unfortunate; no one should be so constrained. The affluent practice contraception. They are not offering advice they do not accept themselves. And the consequences of uncontrolled population growth are visited not upon the rich but upon the poor.

These consequences, it should be noted, come not gradually but with terrible suddenness in the season when the rains fail. As we saw with the potato blight in Ireland, this means that it is the weather, not the preceding population increase, that gets the blame.

However, the problem of population control in the poor country is such as to invite sympathy, not reproach. The most penetrating student of national poverty in our time is the Swedish Nobel Prize winner, Gunnar Myrdal. He is also the most eclectic economist of the age. As a young man he anticipated much of the work of Keynes. His *An American Dilemma* is the classic study of race relations in the United States. Myrdal has shown that the competence of the government of the poor country is itself a part of the equilibrium of poverty. Rich countries have the financial resources to govern effectively. They are not subject to the desperate political pressures of the impoverished. They can make mistakes, for they have a margin for error. The governments of poor countries are politically far more vulnerable. They must assume responsibility for poverty that it is not within their power to ease. They do not have the resources, human or material, to sustain a strong, effective civil service. In consequence, in Myrdal's most famous phrase, there is an intimate association between poverty and the soft state. And nowhere is the softness more inhibiting than in dealing with population growth.

There are exceptions to the rule. China is a very poor country. But, perhaps because of thousands of years of experience in organization, it is not a soft state. And there is no doubt as to the energy with which birth control measures are being pressed. There are stories of committed volunteers who visit each birth-susceptible house before bedtime each evening with the obligatory pill. On the statistics on the effect on population, one's hosts — I was there in 1972 — are less forthcoming. One must be content with assurances that progress is being made.

There is also progress in the Punjab. Nearly twice as large a proportion of all couples has been estimated to use contraceptive protection in that state as in the rest of India. And compulsory sterilization after two or three children is being actively proposed. One must hope that the Chinese and Punjabis will have success and will point the way for all others. For a livable relationship between land and people, control of population is essential.

Expulsion and Migration

The other remedy for overpopulation is for the people to go. This, for centuries, has been the primary solution. It continues to be so. In the last thirty years the need for readjustment between land and people has set in motion great migrations within and into Europe and within the United States. It has attracted only a fraction of the respectable discussion that has been evoked by birth control. That is because the redistribution of people has been from the poor countries or communities to the rich. The rich have not responded with warmth to this remedy. More often, in a mood of some righteousness, they have sought to erect barriers to the tide. They have not wanted to think that a redistribution of population, however logical and effective, is the right answer to the equilibrium of poverty.

It remains, nonetheless, a solution of the greatest social consequence. Neither the pressures in the poor communities nor the tensions in the rich can otherwise be understood. This is most impressively true of the United States. But it is also true of Europe.

In Sutherland in the Scottish Highlands, as we have seen, the equilibrium of poverty was broken by the forthright expulsion of the people and the burning of their villages so they would not return. Agriculture could then be based on wool, not food; this sustained, for the few who remained, a much higher standard of living. Textiles, we saw, worked with double effect. Wool expelled the people; spinning and weaving employed them in the mills to which they went.

The Cotton Equilibrium

It is possible, indeed, that in the last two hundred years the manufacture of clothing has been a greater force for change than the search for food. The textile inventions, along with steam power, made the Industrial Revolution. In 1794, another elementary device changed the social history of the United States. In that year, the Yankee, Eli Whitney, patented a machine, a saw really, for tearing the cotton lint away from the seeds that were imbedded in it. This invention, the cotton gin, and the new spinning and weaving machinery produced both a big supply and a big demand for cotton fiber. Slavery in the Americas had been in decline; it was marginally profitable only for tobacco, sugar and a few other plantation crops. Men who combined compassion with sensitivity to economic need thought it would soon come to an end. Cotton wonderfully restored the slave economy and the slave trade. And, as we saw earlier, it transformed slavery itself from a slightly abhorrent thing to a profoundly beneficent arrangement for protecting the black bondsman from his own inability to cope with this world and for ensuring his salvation in the next. The impact of economics on moral judgment was never more visible and direct.

As the demand for cotton expanded, so did the supply of land for growing it. This was along and back from the lower reaches of the Mississippi, and there the slaves were brought. In the North by the nature of mixed agriculture the farmer worked on a variety of tasks by himself. The fundamental human tendency to relax when out of sight of others was countered by his being an independent proprietor and thus rewarded for his own effort and punished for his own sloth. (In time, this arrangement for inducing effort, the immortal family farm, would also, in the eyes of those associated with it, acquire a transcendental moral value. "We must, at all costs, preserve the American family farm.") To make a cotton crop — cotton is made, not grown — required, in contrast, a much larger labor force. The basic tasks on the plantation, planting which was then by hand, chopping or thinning the plants and picking the cotton, were all done by gangs. The laggard worker could easily be identified. And he could then be encouraged to greater productivity by the voice of the overseer and his whip. There has recently been a grave dispute between economic historians over how frequently slaves were flogged. One greatly controverted study reduces the per-slave average to less than once a year, which could have proved to exceptionally lazy toilers the extreme unwisdom of relying on averages. All do agree that this punishment was a well-regarded incentive. Cotton and slavery were deeply symbiotic.

To the antebellum planter, as we have seen, the slave was a happy, irresponsible child, protected in his innocence by his owner. To the abolitionist, and many since, he was dehumanized, toiling flesh. His enslavement and exploitation saved the planter from the penalties of his own incompetence and from his resulting inability to survive in a free-enterprise world. In a third view the slave was a valuable piece of property, serving with intelligence in a profitable business. As such, he was fed adequately, treated with some decency and given medical care when sick, for this best preserved the capital that he embodied. Free workers at the time were not much better off. It is this last view, recently advanced with supporting claims to measurement, that has been bitterly contested.[2]

In all views there is common ground. The income to the slave was at least as low as the self-interest of the planter allowed. The cotton economy was a forced equilibrium of poverty for all but the very few.

This equilibrium was not altered by the Civil War. With emancipation sharecropping replaced slavery. Before, peonage had legal force. Now it was enforced by the absence of alternatives, and also by various and ingenious arrangements for keeping the sharecropper eternally in debt. Though cotton production was quickly restored — by 1877, it was higher than ever before — the great majority of people associated with its production were still poor. Even if all income had been distributed to the sharecroppers, poverty would still have been acute. The basic relation of people to land was wrong.

The true emancipation came only after World War II. Then machinery and chemistry arrived on the cotton plantation as had the sheep in the Highlands — power cultivation, chemicals to suppress the weeds, the flame cultivator, most important of all the cotton picker. And with these came the remedy, the same in all but detail as in Sutherland and Ireland. There it was the factories or the ships, here it was the highway north. There were jobs in the cities and, if not jobs, welfare checks that would allow for survival. Before World War II, there were 1,466,701 blacks in the rural farm labor force in the states of the Confederacy. In 1970, there were 115,303. In Mississippi, the greatest of the old cotton states, there were 279,176 before the war. In 1970, there were only 20,452.[3] Thus the equilibrium of poverty was broken. The migration is now over, for there are few left to go. People say rightly that the South has changed. Not so many mention the cause.

People caught up in the equilibrium of poverty, people who sense the power of its embrace, search for an escape with great ingenuity, vigor and courage and with very little encouragement from the people in the places to which they seek to go. The rural poor in the United States have been more fortunate than most. They have had some place to which, by entitlement as citizens, they could move. And the South was not the only source of such migrants. There was also Puerto Rico. Here, following its takeover from Spain, the relationship of people to land sustained an equilibrium of poverty that was almost as intractable as in India itself. No journalist visited the island without writing of "the poorhouse of the Caribbean." Then after World War II came the change. Here the cause was less the mechanization of sugar production, which in Puerto Rico was relatively slow, than the airplane and cheap tickets to New York. The people could afford to go, and they went. This, and the development of alternative industry in Puerto Rico itself, broke the old equilibrium. Puerto Rico is still poor but far less so than before migration — before the great and unspoken remedy became available.

Mexico

The Puerto Ricans needed only the price of the cheapest air ticket. The field hands from the South needed even less. To see the importance of migration as a modern remedy one need only go a step farther south to look at an equilibrium of poverty in Mexico where such escape is not easily available.

Mexican independence, we saw, left the landlords undisturbed. In the following decades they thoughtfully increased their holdings at the expense of the ancient communal lands of the people. By 1910, 95 percent of the families in agriculture owned no land. The remaining 5 percent of the families owned nearly half of Mexico; seventeen persons owned nearly a fifth. Some holdings reached sixteen million acres — five times the area of Connecticut.[4] The privileged have regularly invited their own destruction with their greed. In Mexico they were especially brave. Prominent still among the big landowners was the Church. It is a strain on faith if the Church is the landlord and the rents are high. Faith in Mexico was put strongly to the test.

In the long revolution after 1910, the communal lands — the *ejidos* — were returned to the people. Mexico is a large and diverse country; no generalization fits it all. But the usual result was still too many people on too little, too barren land. The familiar problem.

Mexico City was an escape, and it grew prodigiously. But too often it offered only unemployment. The better passage was to Texas, New Mexico, Arizona and California. As in New York for blacks and Puerto Ricans, life would be grim. But it was better than in the overpopulated Mexican village.

So, legally or illegally, they crossed the border. They were called wetbacks for the illegal immigrants who once waded across the Rio Grande. They still wish to come. Employers wish them to come. But a higher social conscience holds they should not come. A large border guard seeks to stop the escape. A man is arrested and sent home. He tries again next day or next week. He is arrested again but on the fifth or sixth try he may make it. No one will doubt the social pressure for this remedy.

It is not, in fact, sufficient. In the Mexican villages the equilibrium of poverty continues. The Mexican Revolution restored the land to the people. But, like the Civil War in the United States, it too left unsolved the far more stubborn problem of the balance between land and people.

The Guest Workers

After World War II, in the years of the great migration from Puerto Rico and the rural South, there was a similar movement, similarly motivated, in Europe. People came to the cities of the industrialized countries from the poor rural villages of Eastern and Southern Europe and adjacent Asia Minor. Yugoslav workers came by the tens of thousands, crossing the line that divides the Communist from the non-Communist world. More would have come from the other Eastern European countries to escape poverty rather than to find liberty, had they been allowed. Turks came to Germany from Asia Minor, Italians and Spaniards to Switzerland, Algerians, Portuguese and some Turks to France.

In all countries a myth was carefully propagated. The movement was for a short time and highly reversible; they were temporary workers, foreign workers, guest workers who would one day go home. No one will now need to be persuaded that something far more fundamental was involved. The guest workers are another chapter in the very long history of the escape from the equilibrium of poverty. Only a determined effort to resist the obvious has kept this from being recognized.

In Britain alone was this great process effectively resisted. West Indians, Pakistanis, Indians, Bengalis, some Africans started to come. But the Empire had been dissolved in the nick of time. One generation had defended it. Their sons defended the home island from its people. Had Britain been protected only by the Rio Grande, they would never have stemmed the tide.

No subject is so lovingly discussed in our time as the economic problem of Britain. No cause is cited with such assurance as the low productivity of her labor force. An obvious explanation goes unmentioned. As compared with Germany and other continental countries, there is no large force of foreign workers impelled to effort by the memory of harder work and greater poverty in the villages whence they came. And impelled also by the fear that, if they relax, they might have to go home. There is satisfaction in Britain over having escaped the social tensions that go everywhere with the migration. Almost no one mentions the economic price. Automobiles must be made, in the main, by Englishmen.

Where It Worked

On the relationship between land and people we have been looking at the hard cases — the dark side of the moon. This is in the established tradition of social study. Only the man who finds everything wrong and expects it to get worse is thought to have a clear brain. (There will be occasion to remark on this again.) Where land and people are involved, there once was a brighter side. It shows, by the contrasting success, the power of this relationship. For me it has also a pleasant, nostalgic value.

It allows me to return to a countryside that I know rather well.

The example is on the north shore of Lake Erie. Its focal point is about midway between Detroit and Buffalo or, by Canadian calculations, between Windsor and Niagara Falls. Port Talbot on Lake Erie may well be the most modest center of water-borne commerce in all the world. There are no piers, no berths, no warehouses, no ships, no unions, no dockers, no pilferage and, for that matter, no harbor and no commerce of any kind. But Port Talbot has its claim on history. From a tiny inlet where, on occasion, a creek runs into the lake the settlement of a large and fertile area of Ontario began.

This was in 1803, when a young Irishman fresh from the King's service arrived on this shore. His name was Thomas Talbot — Colonel Talbot. Having been a good soldier, being highly anglicized and have influence in high places, he had been given a substantial grant of land. He had come to supervise its settlement. Migrants were beginning to arrive from the Scottish Highlands, a race of which the Colonel greatly disapproved. "They make the worst settlers . . . English are the best."[5] But the Scotch, as they called themselves here both then and since, were the available talent. The Clearances again.

Each settler coming to Port Talbot was given fifty acres, were the Colonel in a good mood, attracted to his appearance and sober that day. Business was done through a window in the Colonel's house. Those who made an adverse impression had it shut in their face. For surveying the land in 200-acre lots and laying out the roads, the Colonel then got the other 150 acres. This was in addition to his original grant. As the others flocked in, his estate expanded west toward Windsor and Detroit at a wonderful pace.

Here was the potential for terrible trouble — landlordism on a large scale, the beginning of a North American landed elite. As we've elsewhere seen, nothing would have such lasting effect as this initial distribution of the land. Government would be affected. Political power went with the ownership. Political democracy required, above all, democracy in the possession of the land.

But here democracy was saved. Once their own land was cleared, the settlers wanted the acres next door. They clamored for its purchase. The Colonel had rank but no troops. There were none on which he could call. He could not withstand the pressure, and so he sold. At a nominal price the settlers got the rest of the land. Henceforth there was no irreconcilable issue dividing the haves from the have-nots, the kind of issue that would make democratic government impossible.

It was not an exceptional solution. The land problem in the Middle West and Great Plains in the United States — the 160 acres, and later more, of the Homestead Act — was similarly solved. Likewise in the Canadian West. And here the solution was deliberate. The resulting relationship of people to land allowed of general well-being and made political democracy possible and perhaps inevitable. If all have some wealth, all will want and achieve some share in their government.

With the loss of the land the vision of a new landed aristocracy on Lake Erie also evaporated. Colonel Talbot's ambitions were not in doubt. He built himself a feudal retreat on the height of land above the lake, although only the name — Malahide Castle — had grandeur. The castle was of logs. It was a stopover for well-regarded travelers from England who were not impressed by its comforts. In old age Colonel Talbot traveled himself and visited Napoleon III, apparently as an equal. At midcentury, to protect the line, he made the estate over to his nephew and heir, Colonel Richard Airey. Then came the accident, one of the most disastrous in the long history of military misfortune. In 1852, Colonel Airey was recalled to the colors for the war in the Crimea. It was Richard Airey's name, and no other, that was on the order that dispatched the Light Brigade. Others were to blame but he did not return.

Five or six miles from Port Talbot, to add a further nostalgic word, is the lovely farm to which the Primordial Galbraiths came from Argyll: in my time we still called it the Old Homestead. The sun shone in on it from the south, and the north wind was kept out by a low ridge, and everything ripened a little earlier than anywhere else to the north of the lake. The apples were famous and lovingly discussed. We came for Sunday dinner with a carefully implanted sense of reverence. It was, we knew, an important place.

Of those who settled on such farms none became rich but few were poor. All, within a few years of arrival, a generation at most, had property — farms, houses, barns, livestock, a buggy, furniture, clothing — beyond the dreams of any ancestor in Scotland. From our earliest days we were told that our forebears had been men and women of great courage who had suffered great hardship. The hardship was, in fact, for those who remained in the homeland.

Our farm was three miles away. We had a hundred acres, another fifty up the road. Our purebred Shorthorns were modestly famous, of equable disposition and much admired, especially by their owners, and they led me briefly to a career in animal husbandry. It was in this subject that I took my first degree at the Ontario Agricultural College. My first travel into the United States beyond Detroit was as a member of a team especially accomplished in the judging of livestock. We trained at Michigan State, Purdue and the University of Illinois and competed with marked unsuccess at the International Livestock Exhibition in Chicago. Some have since suggested that I should have remained with this field of knowledge.

I remember our farm also as a lovely place. But I remember without pleasure the exceptionally tedious and repetitive toil. If one is born on a working farm, nothing thereafter ever seems like work.

From such farms and others across the border in the United States there began the last of the great adventures in colonization — the settling of the Canadian West. It is surprisingly recent; when I was a youngster, people were still pulling up stakes (as it was still said) and moving to Manitoba, Saskatchewan and Alberta. The Canadian railroads still had colonist cars — bunks and benches and stoves on which to cook. These, at nominal cost, ferried families to the West.

The Canadian westward movement completed the occupation by Europeans of the empty, grain-growing lands of the world. In the United States, Argentina, Australia and on the Canadian prairies, the Europeans took over. Today, though insignificant in number, they produce an estimated one fifth of the world's breadgrains and a much greater share of the exportable surplus.

In a common view of the world, the poor, densely populated countries of Asia, Africa, Latin America till the soil, work the mines, supply food and raw materials for the industrialized lands of Europe and North America. These are the hewers of wood, the haulers of water, the plowmen for the machine civilization. It's a vision which has little relation to reality. Canada and the United States are large producers of raw materials — lumber, pulp, newsprint, coal, cotton, iron ore and a huge variety of other minerals. And in foods, breadgrains in particular, they are pre-eminent. As the Third World is commonly defined, Canada and the United States are the first of the Third World countries. It is another example of what happens when the conjunction of land and people is fortunate. Where the equilibrium is good, there is well-being; there is also the surplus which helps to feed the people who are caught in the equilibrium that is not good.

The City State

Even from the Ontario countryside some people had to go. There were more in a family than the land could use; had all remained, many would have been poor. Detroit (in addition to the Canadian West) was the salvation. We were patriotic. But our passion for King George V did not survive a five-dollar-a-week wage differential. To absorb extra people, to break thus the equilibrium of rural poverty, is one of the major functions of the modern metropolis. Is this possible?

There is an encouraging case, which is Singapore. It is on the edge of the continent where the equilibrium of rural poverty is most visibly extreme. It lacks all resources, including space. The Singapore state is only 27 miles long and 14 miles wide; a moderately ambulatory citizen can easily cross it on foot in either direction in a day. Along with space, Singapore lacks minerals, materials, food, energy, everything indeed except people and a fortuitous location. It is, all agree, on one of the great ocean crossroads of the world. But being on a crossroad has worked no similar miracle for Panama or Suez. Singapore has a per capita income around eight and a half times that of India, six times that of China. As a place of refuge from rural poverty it works — and far better than Calcutta or Shanghai. There must be a lesson here.

Some of the credit accrues, not surprisingly, to the people. The talents of three races — Chinese, Indians, Malays — are united in a harmonious blend. The people work without the fettering traditions to which they would be subject in the countries from which they or their parents came. Migrants and their immediate descendants always work harder and better than people who have been long settled in their surroundings. To put people down in a new place without accustomed support from land or position, give them the challenge of survival and force them to think may be very cruel but it enormously increases their productivity.

The Singapore government's contribution is to make pragmatic use of all ideas and refuse to be the captive of any one. Is Adam Smith alive in Singapore? The answer is: Very much. There can be few places in the world where pecuniary self-interest is pursued more diligently and with more visible satisfaction in the material result.

Is Keynes there? The answer is also yes. Public outlays are balanced as a matter of course against the availability of workers and the current and prospective capacity of the economy.

The post-Keynesian view of inflation — a view which I have long urged — is also treated with respect in Singapore. Wage settlements are controlled, again as a matter of course, to minimize inflation and to keep Singapore's manufacturing competitive in world markets. When others talk of the need for an incomes policy, Singapore economists, businessmen and union leaders are known to yawn. They've had one for years.

Is there planning, even socialism in Singapore? Have the Webbs, Franklin Roosevelt, Clement Attlee been here? Would Enoch Powell and Barry Goldwater be distressed? The answer again is yes. If housing, harbor works, transportation and industrial sites are needed, the government provides. Public apartment blocks control the horizon. Self-interest serves well as a motivation. But it is recognized in Singapore that it does not serve all purposes. And it serves best within a framework of systematic and deliberate planning.

Some of the success of Singapore must be attributed to the rule that nothing is good or bad in principle. The test is whether it works or helps people to work. There can be few countries so little interested in ideological dispute, so free from the rhetoric of both free enterprise and socialism. This is an aesthetic treat.

Singapore has a lively intellectual and university life; the best in the East outside Japan. It is not a place of fear. But it is not a place of perfect freedom. The unions are subject to the wage restraints just mentioned. There is little sympathy for anything that seems to interfere with work. The government gives no encouragement to those who suggest that the Chinese in China have a model that should be emulated. Even travel to China by the young is discouraged. I do not applaud such caution. It seems unnecessary; in any case, there are some principles that all must defend. But the larger point is clear. Singapore shows that there is an urban solution to the problem of land and people. Many people can, indeed, live well on little space.

It is not a secure or easy solution. Singapore must have friendly, well-disposed neighbors, and it must be secure in its trade with the world at large. Much depends also on the continuing tolerant good sense of the people and the ability of the government to adapt. Change anywhere in the world — recession, inflation, alterations in the trade routes — affects Singapore. It cannot influence such changes; being small and without power, it must always adjust. This adjustment must be governed by thought, not formula. It cannot be defeated by narrow political interest or passion. The people must have the confidence, good nature and sense of community to accept change, including when it hurts.

Singapore must also master the increasingly intricate and costly problems of the great metropolis. That is a different and very difficult task.

11.
The Metropolis

So, in the end, almost everyone goes to the city. Whatever the beginning, it is to this that the industrial civilization comes. Better even than the size or composition of the national product, the extent of urbanization measures that development. At the beginning of the present century 38 percent of American workers were employed in agriculture. By 1975, it was 4 percent. In Britain it was 2.5 percent. By contrast, in Italy the agricultural labor force is still around 16 percent of the total; in India some 72 percent are employed, underemployed or unemployed on farms.[1]

Since it is there that people live, the problems of the industrial civilization are seen as the problems of the city. What should be blamed on expanding income and output, the changing composition of product, higher and different consumption, the modern role of unions, the unwillingness of people peacefully to starve gets blamed instead on the way the city is governed. The modern big-city mayor is a most convenient figure in our time. He gets, and in his innocence largely accepts, the responsibility for the tensions, discomforts, maladjustments and failures of the industrial system.

It follows that to understand that system nothing is so important as an understanding of its urban life. This, like most things, must be examined in some historical depth. For the word city itself, in its singular form, is misleading. There is not one kind of city but several, and all are combined, in varying mix and form, in the great metropolis. Four different types are readily recognizable: the Political Household, the Merchant City, the Industrial City and the Camp. These together make the modern Metropolis.

The Political Household

The Political Household, for most of time, has been the extension of the dwelling of a ruler. Like his palace, it was an expression of his taste and personality and a manifestation of the grandeur of his realm. Visitors spoke of the elegance (or more rarely of the modesty) of the ruler's palace. They spoke as frequently of the magnificence or, on occasion, the squalor of his capital.

Mostly it was the magnificence. Over the centuries nothing has been so thought to enhance royal personality, competence in armed slaughter apart, as the architectural embellishment of the seat of government. Rome, Persepolis, Angkor, Constantinople, Paris, Versailles, the Forbidden City, Leningrad née St. Petersburg, Vienna, Segovia and literally a hundred other wonders are the result. The late Joseph A. Schumpeter of Harvard, a man who rejoiced in awkward or unpalatable truth, enjoyed remarking on the migration each summer of the tens of thousands of resolutely democratic

Americans to see the architectural wonders of the Old World. Their attention during these months, he noted, would be centered exclusively on the monuments to past despotism.

The ruler imposed his will and therewith his order on the Political Household. The order itself was important. Symmetry, even without taste or imagination, has some claim upon the eye. Disorder, a point of importance when we come to the Industrial City, has none. But also, and more often than might have been imagined, there was a conjunction between power, imagination and taste. One of the most remarkable results of that combination has been kept intact for four hundred years. Not only has it survived but it is unsullied; unlike Leningrad or Florence or Paris there is no commercial or industrial overlay or extension through which the visitor must peer or pick his way. The city, the archetype of the Political Household in its high royalist aspect, is Fatehpur Sikri. It has rightly been called "the world's most perfectly preserved ghost town."[2]

Fatehpur Sikri

It was built by Akbar the Great on a low rocky ridge twenty-four miles from Agra, one of the inspired capitals of the Moghuls. (Delhi and Lahore were yet others.) The legend, possibly more trustworthy than most, is that the site was chosen because there in a village lived a holy man, Shaikh Salim Chishti, whom Akbar the Great had visited when he was in despair because he had no son and heir, his near infinity of wives notwithstanding. A son, named Salim for the saint and later to succeed his father as Jahangir, was then forthcoming. In gratitude Akbar, around 1571, quarried the ridge, made a lake some twenty miles around and built a new capital. Visitors coming from Europe in the next years found a city larger than London and in its public buildings by a wide margin more elegant. Fourteen years later Akbar moved on. There are various solemn explanations for this — a failure of the water supply, a strategically unsatisfactory location. The explanations overlook the most plausible reason: other rulers tired of a palace and moved on; the Moghuls, as a legacy perhaps of their nomadic antecedents in central Asia, tired of a city and left.

When Akbar left, so did the people. The private dwellings and shops decayed and disappeared. The walls, mosques, mint, treasury, caravansary, palaces and other public buildings remained. No commerce, no industry has since come near. The ridge that Akbar converted to his capital was of rich salmon-red sandstone. This became the palaces and walls; frequently it was cut and assembled as though it were timbers and boards so that one thinks of wood structures made of stone. In the clean, dry air and hot sun this marvelous material mellowed but did not crumble or decay. So at Fatehpur Sikri we can see in the purest possible form the city that I have called the Political Household.

Almost everything that survives — the single and double columns that make up the basic design, their massive capitals, the medley of great and small domes, the mosque, the tolerant combination of

Hindu and Islamic decoration in the quarters of the Hindu queen, the towering Victory Gate with its enigmatic quotation: "The world is a bridge, pass over it but do not build upon it" — is symmetrically a part of the larger whole. That this city was the extension of one man's personality is not in doubt.

The elegance and symmetry of the Political Household are important for the pleasure they give. This is important also because from the Political Household, along with the Merchant City, comes the image we still retain of what a city should be. From it also has come an important convention in modern urban architecture and design. It is the belief that government has a special claim to architectural and urban magnificence. Industrialists are expected to work, even though they do not themselves live, in cities of routine squalor. Their office buildings may be tall but they must be functional. Executive offices may be large and expensively furnished but only because cost/benefit analysis shows that the resulting impression pays off. Politicians and public officials are believed to need elegance for its own sake. The capital in which they work should be planned and its buildings embellished, even though in a depraved way, as were the royal palaces. What rejoices the eye must, at a minimum, be balanced with what distresses the taxpayer. Aberration at great cost — the Rayburn Building on Capitol Hill, the new FBI fortress on Pennsylvania Avenue, the Woolworth-Gothic towers of the Stalin era in Moscow, the Rockefeller elephantiasis in Albany — is briefly deplored and then forgiven.

The Political Household places its stamp on the city hall and civic center of the modern city. But its influence is most strongly reflected in the modern planned capital — Washington, New Delhi, Canberra, Brasilia, Islamabad, all cities that reflect a ruling conception and design. It deserves a thought that these are almost the only wholly modern cities that the present-day tourist ever believes worth a visit.

The Merchant City

The Merchant City had also a unity of conception and design. This was less the result of central authority than unity of taste. Merchants must be sensitive to fashion. At any given time in architecture, as in dress, manners or crime, there is a ruling style. This gave unity to the houses of the merchants. Also the merchant communities in the mercantilist era before the Industrial Revolution had a strong sense of their collective interest. This led to a meticulous regulation of the terms and conditions of trade and the antecedent manufacture. The regulation extended naturally to the plan of the towns, the design of the houses. Within this larger framework there was then a rewarding competition. The quality and style of the house was an advertisement of the quality and style of the merchant therein, the merchandise therefrom. In consequence, the Merchant Cities — Venice, Genoa, Amsterdam, the Hansa towns that survived the bombers of World War II — rival in order and elegance the

Political Households.

The architecture and design differed not in quality but in its reflection of the central purpose of the city. Its supreme expressions in the older Political Household were the palaces of the ruler. In the Merchant City it was inevitably the houses of the merchants, the guild hall and the town hall. To these, on occasion, were added the cathedral or church, for these advertised, legitimized and, in some measure, sanctified the gains from trade.

Two great Merchant Cities survive, as does Fatehpur Sikri, with little modern clutter. One, of course, is Venice, the greatest and by far the best-preserved of all museums of civic design. The other, less well known but more easily encompassed and comprehended, is Bruges in Belgium. It was a member of the Hanseatic League, which was also a source of common ideas in civic design, and in the fourteenth century it was considered the northern counterpart of Venice itself. It is intact because of two accidents — the silting up of the river Zwin which separated it for four hundred years from the sea and thus from the ravages of progress, and the heaven-sent accident in 1914 - 18 which left it a mere twenty miles removed but totally untouched by the guns of the bloodiest battles of all time. Bruges and its beautiful companions of the mercantile era have also left a deep imprint on our thinking about the city.

We still assess the quality of a city by the elegance and glitter of its principal shopping streets. We do not accept that department stores and shops can be strictly functional; the first must have a certain residual grandeur and the second a modicum of style. Somewhat similar standards are brought to bear on the modern shopping center; its distinction increases if not with its beauty, then with its size, ostentation and apparent cost. When the shops of the central city decay or close up, even though branches are burgeoning on the traffic exchanges on the edge of town, the whole city is said to be in decline. Our tendency to test the quality or distinction of an urban community by its shopping districts is one of the continuing legacies of the Merchant City.

The Merchant City is now part of the Metropolis. Only in a subdued and degraded form, related not to ships and the sea but to agriculture, can the modern Merchant City be found in pure form. It is the onetime crossroads in Iowa, East Anglia and Normandy to which farmers repair for fertilizer, farm machinery, building materials, clothing and the education of their young. Its most ubiquitous mercantile establishment is the automobile service station. Merchants still live in the largest houses back from the road and behind a wall or lawn. But there is an aspect of shabby impermanence about these retreats — flaking paint, loose shutters, unraked leaves. It is because the occupants are now civil servants, the current managers of J. C. Penney, Sears, Marks & Spencer. One day soon they will be moved along. The modern Merchant City in its pure form is a depleted and trivial reminder of its great precursors.

The Industrial City

With the Industrial Revolution the Industrial City became synonymous with the city. In consequence, the very connotation of the word city changed. Before 1776, the word had an overtone of grandeur. Dick Whittington's first glimpse of London was of the promised land. Dr. Johnson was even more affirmative: "No, Sir, when a man is tired of London, he is tired of life; for there is in London all that life can afford." The American Republic was launched in Philadelphia, then the second largest city in the English-speaking world. It was regarded by all as beautifully planned and admirably built, and what was then built is so regarded today. This was near the end of urban beauty; soon thereafter a reference to a city became a reference to something not grand, not beautiful, not even solid but something mean, ill-built and dirty. The Industrial City became the characteristic city, and all cities came to be thought somewhat sordid.

There was much about the Industrial

City which helped assure this reputation. The Political Household housed courtiers, courtesans, civil servants, soldiers and servants. In the Merchant City were clerks, petty officials, tradesmen. In both of these pre-Industrial Cities there were craftsmen, artisans, small shopkeepers and an abundance of mendicants. But, with the exception of the mendicants, most of those who lived in these cities were required to be generally presentable. That was because they served people of professed gentility who might be repelled by unduly crude appearance, manner or aroma. With the different occupations went a pleasing variety in dress, speech and personal style.

The Industrial City, by contrast, made no such demands. People were now a servo-mechanism. That service was not diminished in the slightest by their being shabby, unwashed, rough of manner and ripe of smell. On the whole, these characteristics were approved, for they minimized the expense of maintenance. In the Industrial City men sought, above all, the lowest cost. The reasons were not entirely to be deplored; the Industrial City, unlike its predecessors, served cheaply those who were also poor.

The people of the Industrial City were not beautiful. Nor were their dwellings. Nor, a commonplace point, were the processes by which their goods were made. These all but uniformly involved much smoke and grime. Coal had to be dug and washed; ore had to be smelted; locomotives had to be fired; steam engines had to be fueled; these were all necessary even for processes that otherwise were clean. So almost all industrial operations nurtured or spread filth. Amidst the valuable modern concern over the effect of industrial growth on the environment few note that the course of industrial progress has involved a remarkably steady march from the foul process to the relatively pure one — from dirty coal to clean gas, oil and electricity; from smoke-filled foundries to automated processes and air-conditioned control rooms; from belching steam engines to cleaner internal combustion engines and the wholly antiseptic electric motor, the ultimate power plant of which is far more carefully monitored for pollution than the multitude of chimneys it replaced. Indeed, we take it for granted that the older the industrial community or the more obsolescent the factory, the dirtier it all will be. The early processes firmly established the reputation of the Industrial City as a dirty place.

Finally, among the constants of the Industrial City were the industrialists. While a merchant had to be a man of style and taste, not so a manufacturer. His concern was with methods and machines and efficiency; for coal, steel, chemicals, machinery, the buyer was concerned not with charm, only with performance and cost. And the early consumer products of the Industrial City — cloth and more cloth, cheap tin trays — made no demands on taste. So the early manufacturer was like his product, solid, efficient and graceless, where not crude. He built his house above the mills. Unlike the merchant's house it was expected to be ungainly if not hideous. Economic determinism is omnipresent and extends itself strongly to art.

The Birminghams

Not all Industrial Cities were alike. The leading industrialists impressed themselves strongly upon the life of the city, and sometimes to its advantage. Retiring in 1874 as the world's most eminent manufacturer of screws, Joseph Chamberlain was thrice mayor of Birmingham, England. There followed a remarkable burst of civic pride and enthusiasm. Slums were cleared, parks established, a library and art gallery created, the water and gas supply taken into municipal ownership, sanitation and health made a civic concern. The city that, after Manchester, epitomized English industry became a model of urban development and administration for all the kingdom.

It was, alas, the exception. By the turn of the century in the United States its namesake in Alabama was on its way to becoming the leading Industrial City of the South. It was much nearer the mode.

Coal, iron ore and limestone were all there in close proximity. They were brought together by the Tennessee Coal and Iron Company which, in 1907, was brought by J. P. Morgan into the United States Steel Corporation. The result was absentee management twice removed. The Steel Corporation was operated for Morgan by Elbert Henry Gary, of whom it was said that he never saw a blast furnace until after his death. This Birmingham was merely a place of work. In the early nineteen-twenties, as elsewhere in the American steel industry, men worked a twelve-hour day and a seven-day week, and Christmas like Sunday was just another day of toil. The Alabama Birmingham still bears the simple imprint of its industrial origins. Until recent times its principal expression of civic pride was in its firm resistance to racial integration. However, nothing, even when bad, is forever. Of late, this Birmingham too has moved on to pride in its hospitals, its other civic facilities and its athletic teams.

In one extreme variant of the Industrial City the industrialist took full responsibility for inception, design and administration. He laid out streets, built and owned the houses, built and operated the store or stores where people shopped and sometimes were required to shop. And he laid on water supply and sewerage, if any. This, as in the cities of the princes, was an imposed order, an industrial household. It was, however, designed not for grandeur but for economy and to ensure that the inmates, however sullen, would not be mutinous. A rewarding calm was enforced by keeping them permanently in debt to their employer who could expel them on demand from their houses. It seems possible that no experiment in controlled social design was ever so uniformly reviled as this, the company town. When all was quiet, the employer-landlord would sometimes be celebrated by his sycophants as a Christian idealist or a genial and wise paternalist, and sometimes he would believe his notices. Then, in moments of truth and high ceremony, he would be hung in effigy by people who deplored only the need for the substitution.

The Economics of the City

The government of the Industrial City reflected admirably the dominant economic ethic — the belief in self-interest and classical laissez-faire. There was a city government; it was operated on loose leash from the local capitalists. Since city services added to taxes and living costs and led ultimately to the diminution of profit or the enhancement of production expense, they were kept to the minimum. The filth of the industry was mingled with the offal of the inhabitants. Streets need not be lighted for toilers who should be asleep. The factories required only an unlettered proletariat so that was what the schools provided. Again the imprint of economics on culture.

The Industrial City in Europe in the last century was better served than its counterpart in the United States. Those elected or appointed to office were usually nonlarcenous. In the United States men were measured in straightforward fashion by the money they made. City officials, not surprisingly, sought also to show their worth; this they did by appropriating public money, sometimes in some decently circuitous fashion, for themselves. In 1888, Lord Bryce, the first great British student of American political institutions and folkhabits, concluded that the "government of cities is the one conspicuous failure of the United States."[3] Two decades later Lincoln Steffens, then the dean of the American muckrakers, a man with a unique capacity for repetition, told at appalling length of the evil association of reputable economic power and disreputable political power in the American metropolis. Neither Bryce nor Steffens should have been surprised. The city that so distressed these observers corresponded precisely to industrial need. The industrialist was free from restraint. He could do as he needed with air, water, landscape. The city sheltered his work stock at the lowest possible cost. Since he owned the politicians, they were reliably in his service. Given that the purpose of the city was to produce goods cheap, nothing more was to be asked or expected.

As the visible face of the industrial

civilization in the leading industrial countries — Britain, Germany, the United States — the Industrial City had its sharpest delineation around the beginning of the present century. Sheffield, Essen, Pittsburgh were its purest form. Since then in the older countries the image has again been blurred. A new city — the Camp — has appeared. And this and all of the antecedent cities have melted into the Metropolis.

The Camp

A most important influence for urban change has been money, rising real income. In the Industrial City this, in time, was reflected in the housing and even more in the shops, shopping centers, cinemas and stadia where incomes were spent. The social power of money is great for the rich but also for others as well. With higher income came a much enhanced professional class — doctors, lawyers, accountants. Also a new race of artisans, surgeons to automobiles, television sets, washing machines, electricity and the plumbing. And, as we've seen, the industrial firm itself no longer consisted of only an owner, a few bookkeepers, a few foremen and a large toiling mass. Instead there was a complex superstructure: sales managers, advertising managers, controllers and those who understand the computers. Along with the bankers, lawyers, advertising men and public relations flaks who serve the industrial establishment, these made up a new and sizable layer between workers and owners. They were joined by the expanding white-collar mass who, in the industrial nations, now far outnumber those who run the machines. The servo-proletariat of the Industrial City has been submerged in the great and growing artisan, clerical, technical, professional and managerial class.

With the Industrial City came a well-founded desire by the few who could afford it to escape its smoke and grime and unlovely landscape and, even more, its inhabitants. So with the Industrial City came the suburb. With the reconstitution of a mercantile class and the appearance of the new managerial elite, the number who could afford this escape increased greatly. In the suburbs the rich or the modestly affluent could live in comparatively clean air with their private trees and grass. And they could have schools, churches and recreational facilities of superior quality, the quality ensured and the cost kept down by their not being shared with the poor. There could also be a rewarding segregation according to income, occupation or race. There were rich suburbs and moderate-income suburbs, those favored by bankers and stockbrokers, those that excluded the Jews. In time, every sizable city was surrounded by these classified enclaves.

Unlike the Political Household, the Merchant City or the Industrial City itself, these settlements had no central political or economic function; they did not govern, sell or make. They were merely places where people found space and lived. Increasingly, given the peripatetic character of the modern organization man, the space was occupied only for a brief time. In the absence of central function and the impermanence of its residents, the modern suburb is often less a city than a bivouac. Thus its name: the Camp. In the United States there is yet another Birmingham, this one a bivouac for the peripatetic affluent from Detroit.

Migration

In the classical Industrial City the working force grew, procreation apart, in response to two forces. One was the attraction of the wages of its mills, however dark and satanic. The second was because of the compelled correction of the imbalance between land and people. The people had nowhere else to go. The Industrial Cities of late-eighteenth-century Britain attracted workers with a wage which, however low, was better than could be had in agriculture. However idyllic, Auburn was a very low-income place. And simultaneously the Acts of Enclosure and in Scotland the already-noticed Clearances, along with an increasing population, were liquidating even that alternative. "Industry was in fact the only refuge for thousands of men who found themselves cut off from their traditional occupations."[4] People, a contemporary petition moaned, are being "driven from necessity and want of employ, in vast crowds, into manufacturing towns, where the very nature of their employment, over the loom or forge, may waste their strength, and consequently debilitate their posterity."[5] English agriculture was substituting the greater intelligence, energy and economics of the large-scale farmer for the inefficient, labor-intensive husbandry of those who worked small plots and shared the common land. Seventy-five years later, as we've also seen, the rural population of Ireland was expelled to the Industrial Cities (and also to mines and railway construction camps) in the United States, again by agricultural change. In the same and subsequent years there was a great and accelerating movement to the United States, Canada and South America from Northern, Eastern and Southern Europe, much of it to the vacant lands but increasingly also to the Industrial Cities. After World War II came the aborted migration from the erstwhile Empire to

Britain, from the less to the more industrialized European countries and from south to north in the United States. Of these migrations and their causes the last chapter has told.

With these waves of immigrants the city underwent a further change. Previously it had been taken for granted that its internal tensions were those of the industrial society. The workers confronted the capitalist. The strike was its overt manifestation. The people in the valley went into the streets in angry opposition to the employer on the hill and his housecarls in the police. After weeks, sometimes months of struggle, sometimes with violence, always with deprivation, one side or the other gave in. Work was resumed but the anger persisted. This was the conflict that was thought basic in all industrial society.

With the rise of the new managerial class, negotiations with the workers passed from owners to organization men. The organization men could be blamed for strikes; better managers avoided or negotiated out of conflict. Those who bargained did not themselves pay the higher wages that were the cost of the settlement. Not having to pay makes a difference. The modern industrial firm was powerful in its markets so, after some ceremonial acrimony, it could pass higher wage costs along to the public in higher prices. Strikes still occurred. But now they were mostly without rancor. Sometimes they usefully reduced burdensome business inventories.

But with migration a new conflict appeared. That was between the two proletariats of the Industrial City, between the old, established, relatively secure, relatively well-paid working force and the new dark tide which it perceived as being both socially and economically its nemesis. Suspicion and dislike were, as often before, facilitated by differences in color, language or country of origin. For the new migrants the capitalist was no longer the enemy. Many who cleaned the streets, tended the buildings and labored without skill on construction sites wished they had industrial employment. Many others simply wished they had employment. Or housing, schools or transportation or a society that was decently color-blind. Their enemy was the government or the social order which resented their presence and sought their exclusion from schools, politics and social life. When these inhabitants revolted, they did not wish to burn the capitalist; they sought, logically, to burn the city.

In Britain prior to the arrival of the Pakistanis, Indians and West Indians, race prejudice — racial xenophobia — had been thought an American disorder. And, in the Northern United States, it had long been thought a Southern affliction. Following the great migrations it was discovered to be pandemic. It also ran in Switzerland against Italians, in Germany against Turks. This tension and the thought and action it provokes are the most dramatic and debated urban development of modern times. On this I will have a further word presently.

The Metropolis

The diversification of the modern city caused by rising incomes and the changing structure of industry, the arrival of the new immigrants and the growth of the Camps have created the final type of city. As noted, it draws on and unites all the kinds that have gone before. It might be called the post-Industrial City; more simply it is the Metropolis. Industry can still be a major *raison d'etre* and often is. But the old class structure of the Industrial City has ceased to exist. So have the physical lineaments of the factory town. Affluence has brought the shops and shopping centers and the ancillary services that are in descent from those of the Merchant City. Around, about and forming a part of the Metropolis are the Camps. All have a governing nucleus, which is the residue of the Political Household. In the greatest of the Metropolises — London, Paris, Rome, Tokyo, New York (with the United Nations) — this still has an important bearing on its character.

When we ask as to the future of the modern Metropolis, we are asking about the future of the modern industrial society, for the Metropolis is its tangible, visible expression.

The assimilation of the new arrivals will be the easiest of the problems of the modern Metropolis. The scale of this movement in modern times has been very large. At least within the United States it will be smaller in the future; a country can only liquidate its agricultural working force once. And much tension that is attributed to race is really the result of the unsettling effects of the inward movement and of the economic and cultural poverty of the countryside in which the people were reared.

In the nineteen-thirties, the movement of a very poor agricultural population from the southern Great Plains into California, the Okies and Arkies of John Steinbeck's great novel, was the source of major social tension. Like the subject peoples of Eastern Europe the Okies and Arkies were, when clean, indubitably white. Nonetheless they were pictured as a race apart. Their children are now indistinguishable from other Californians. So it will be with the children, or at most the grandchildren, of the recent migrants. They will have higher educational and economic aspirations than their parents or grandparents. These aspirations, in greater or less measure, they will achieve. When this happens, the problems of race and color will diminish and even seem archaic. The rich and the poor of the same language, color and race do not live easily side by side. The affluent of different races usually live quite peaceably with one another.

The more plausible problem of twenty or thirty years hence will be how to arrange a new migration into the cities. For, as the present generation of urban dwellers moves up the ladder, there will be a demand for someone to do the less agreeable jobs that they leave behind.

Where Capitalism Fails

On two other matters the prospect is more grim. First there is the fact that capitalism performs excellently in providing those things — automobiles, disposable packaging, drugs, alcohol — that cause problems for the city. But it is inherently incompetent in providing the things that city dwellers most urgently need. Capitalism has never anywhere provided good houses at moderate cost. Housing, it seems unnecessary to stress, is an important adjunct of a successful urban life. Nor does capitalism provide good health services, and when people live close together with attendant health risks, these too are important. They are made more urgent because, on coming to the city, people no longer accept as inevitable untended sickness and then a quiet death as they would in some lonesome sharecropper's cabin. Nor does capitalism provide efficient transportation for people — another essential of the life of the Metropolis.

In Western Europe and Japan the

failure of capitalism in the fields of housing, health and transportation is largely, though not completely, accepted. There industries have been intensively socialized. In the United States there remains the conviction that, however contrary the experience, private enterprise will eventually serve. To assert the inherently public character of these industries, even though the practice affirms it, still seems radical. Nothing is now so important as to agree that the nature of these services *is* public and then to ensure that their performance is not merely a matter of adequacy but of pride. City life will never be good while housing, health care and transportation are poor.

There is a larger need. That is to see far more clearly than at present the essentially social character of the Metropolis. In its days of greatest elegance, the city was a household, an extension of the domestic arrangements of the ruler. No line then separated private from public tasks. Construction, artistic embellishment and maintenance of the city — what would now be regarded as public tasks — may well have absorbed the larger share of the aggregate public and private income. With the Industrial City it came to be assumed that payment for public tasks — education, police protection, courts, sanitation, recreation, public entertainment, care of the old and impoverished — would be only a small subtraction from total revenue. The private household, no one doubted, had the major claim.

This continues to be the assumption. The consequences all recognize. Among the affluent and even among the poor, services supplied out of private income are far more amply endowed than those provided by the city. Houses are clean, streets are filthy. Personal wealth expands; there are too few police officers to protect it. Television sets are omnipresent; schools are deficient. Bathing is possible in a private bathroom but not safely at a public beach. Where capitalism is efficient, it adds to the public tasks of the city; it increases the number of automobiles that must be accommodated in and through the city, adds to the detritus that must be picked up from the streets and makes progressively more difficult the problem of keeping breathable the air and sustaining a minimum tranquility of life.

This is another way of saying that the social aspect of modern metropolitan life is extremely expensive, far more expensive than we have yet imagined. The notion that these social costs are only a deduction from total public and private expenditure — a view that is a legacy of the attitudes of the Industrial City — is now obsolete. It may well be in the future that, if the Metropolis is to be pleasant, healthy, otherwise agreeable and culturally and intellectually rewarding, public expenditures will have to be higher than private expenditures.

The test is to look at the Metropolis as one would look at a household and, indeed, as the rulers regarded the Political Household. There is no *a priori* case for one class of expenditures, public or private, over another — for street sweepers over vacuum cleaners, schools over television sets. The question is which returns the greatest satisfaction at the margin and serves best the sense of the community as to what is good. If the satisfaction from public services is higher than that from private goods for the typical urban dweller, there will obviously be more social good in accepting the fact than in resisting it. Not ideology but the social character of the Metropolis is the controlling circumstance.

The acceptance of the social character of the Metropolis involves more than questions of bread and butter, of housing, health care, clean streets and safe parks. It also involves another dimension, that of art and design. This is my last point. We've seen that people travel by the millions to view the Political Households and Merchant Cities of the past. And many also go to see Washington, Canberra, New Delhi and Brasilia. They do not visit, even in their present and improved manifestations, any of the three Birminghams. The difference is elementary. The Political Households were conceived as a unity. Their design was envisaged as a whole. The cities which people forswear carry the aesthetic legacy of classical liberal capitalism. There is no proof that people were more sensitive to artistic need in the days of Dresden or St. Petersburg than in the age of Düsseldorf or Pittsburgh. But Dresden and St. Petersburg were faithful to their central conception and their common style. These were enforced as the architect enforces a common conception for a whole house. This concept can be good or bad. But one rule can be laid down as final: whether good or bad, it will be better than when there is no governing order at all.

As a legacy of classical liberalism there is a marked unwillingness to socialize design, to specify overall architectural styles to which the subordinate units must conform. It is an unjust interference with property rights and personal preference. But there is no place where the substitution of social for classical liberal expression is more urgent and where, paradoxically, the result serves better the classical utilitarian goal of the greatest good for the greatest number.

The interference with property rights is real. One solution lies in extending the public ownership of urban land. This too accords with the inherently social character of the city and the inescapably socialist character of housing. I've long wondered why European socialists or American liberals, when gathering on occasions of high ceremony to affirm their faith, give so little attention to the public ownership of urban land. For no other form of property is the public case so clear.

The Tyranny of Circumstance

To speak of the social character of the Metropolis and of the necessarily socialist character of its important services is to arouse instant suspicion. There is advocacy here. A socialist is speaking. The proper discounts should be applied.

To suspect advocacy in such matters is not a bad precaution but it is not appropriate in this case. As often in these matters, we imagine choice — scope for ideological preference — when, in fact, there is little or none. The social character of the Metropolis derives not from preference. It follows, as earlier noted, from the far harder circumstance that millions of people live in close proximity to each other with all the friction, all the antisocial opportunity, all the social needs that this ordains. It is this that forces upon the city its social character. This is not the product of preference. It is, once again, the tyranny of circumstance.

Had one wished to forestall this tyranny, there would have been only one way. That would have been to forestall the people. The Metropolis should have been aborted long before it became New York, London or Tokyo.

12.
Democracy, Leadership, Commitment

Man, at least when educated, is a pessimist. He believes it safer not to reflect on his achievements; Jove is known to strike such people down. Dangers, uncompleted tasks, failures remain in his mind.

Still, in the last two hundred years some remarkable things have been accomplished. Millions now escape poverty, live more contentedly and much longer than ever before. The decline of religious faith in our time proceeds partly from the fact that so many get so much more out of this world and feel it possible in consequence to repose less hope in the next. White men no longer believe they were meant by nature or sent by heaven to rule those who are black, brown or yellow. No one, two hundred years ago, could have foreseen man's capacity, public, social and corporate, to organize for such vast and intricate tasks as arranging travel to the moon, getting oil from under the North Sea or making a television series. Adam Smith thought the joint-stock company — the corporation, in modern language — doomed to incompetence and failure because it taxed this capacity for cooperation beyond feasible limits. Maybe we even understand war better than in the heroic days. Personal proficiency in killing is no longer praised so fulsomely as in earlier times. Being killed is not thought quite so transcendent a glory. Both are recommended, even for other people, with some slight diffidence.

Our tendency, however, is to reflect on failure. We remind ourselves of the number of people who are still poor in the poor countries and also in the rich. We reflect that, two hundred years after Adam Smith, economists have achieved not the control of inflation, not the prevention of unemployment, but the ability to have both at the same time. Organization — the capacity for cooperative effort — we note, can get us to the moon but not into and around New York. Our perception of war now includes the ability to destroy all life if war comes.

Perhaps this pessimism is good. I certainly think so. It causes us to ask: "Well, what can I do?" It is a good question. Is there anything the individual can do?

But there is a prior question. Social existence, as we have sufficiently seen, is a continuing process. As one of its problems is solved, others emerge, often from the previous solutions themselves. Our habit is to ask for solutions. The very best ones will be only a temporary achievement, although nobody should minimize the importance of that. We need also to spare a thought for the mechanism by which we tackle the flow of problems which, like waves on the beach, will continue to come. How good, in particular, are the mechanisms of democratic government for this continuing task? And what makes them better or worse? That I perceive to be the task to which this small adventure in ideas ultimately comes.

The Swiss Case

More than twenty years ago I was working on a book, and it was going badly. I sought out a small Swiss village in the Bernese Oberland, secluded myself and, out of boredom, thought each afternoon, evening and much of the night of what I would write the next morning. The results by accepted standards were excellent; the book, *The Affluent Society,* was held, not least of all by me, to be useful. I've been returning to Switzerland and to Gstaad to write ever since. I've become a part-time Swiss professor; a librarian at the Swiss national library told me some years ago, to my satisfaction, that I was being reclassified as a semi-Swiss author. I've come to feel that I know this small country moderately well.

The Swiss example has always encouraged me to believe that there is power and effectiveness in democracy. It is the Swiss instinct that problems can be solved by the collective responsibility and intelligence of the people themselves. It is that responsibility and intelligence that count. Accordingly, the solution lies with the citizen, not the leader. The Swiss citizen does not delegate to the great in the belief that they have the answers. He seeks the answers. In a few of the 22 (very recently 23) cantons, all voters still meet as a legislative body. The initiative and referendum — a direct vote on issues — are much used. In consequence, many more elections are to resolve issues than to choose leaders. In further consequence, the Swiss have had few noted leaders, few heroes. The most famous Swiss was Calvin, who was French. After Calvin comes William Tell, whose distinction rests only on a somewhat perilous approach to parental duty.

One winter day a few years ago a telephone message was relayed to me from a man in Bern whose name seemed familiar; he wanted me to come over for lunch to discuss economic problems. I sought out my very intelligent Swiss neighbor to find out who he was. "He might have been last year's President," she said. "Anyway, I'm quite sure he isn't President now."

Small countries are far from being masters of their people's destiny. Inflation and recession come in from abroad. In a nuclear war these countries would be no less the victims than the nuclear powers themselves. But for questions within the power of the Swiss democracy — protection of the environment; ethnic reconciliation between those who speak German, French, Italian; a tolerant relationship between religions; provision of good housing and public services; sensible support to agriculture and industry; education that nurtures the democratic idea — it has found solutions, brilliant solutions on the whole.

It is common, even there, to dismiss this democratic accomplishment by saying that Switzerland is a small country that also has had no wars. Perhaps it was the good sense of Swiss democracy that kept it out of Europe's internecine wars, as some have called them. To say that a small country has no problems shows only an instinct for error. Ulster is a small country. So is Lebanon. So is Chile. The Belgians quarrel dutifully over language. Small countries may feel especially obliged to assert their capacity for self-destruction. It is a form of compensation.

For the task of governing themselves, the Swiss have three sources of strength. Each participant in the democracy has a personal concern for the result. Small size and the continued protection of the authority and autonomy of the canton and the responsibilities of the commune or local government — the celebrated Swiss federalism — is a help. One person's vote and voice can have an appreciable bearing on the outcome. So they are worth using and worth careful thought. Important issues are submitted to the people in referendum. Indeed, as noted, most Swiss elections are to pass on issues (new taxes, new spending, votes for women, limits on the number of foreign workers) and are not, as elsewhere, to select between parties and politicians.

The next source of strength is the Swiss sense of community. The Swiss, one need hardly say, have a keen sense of personal pecuniary interest. But they recognize the greater loss if the community is sacrificed to the special interest. Meeting politicians, businessmen, trade union leaders, even bankers in Switzerland over the years, I've always been impressed by the feeling, implied or expressed, that the interest of the commune, canton or country has precedence over the interest of the individual, party or organization and that this is not generosity but good sense.

Finally, I've always thought that the Swiss were far more interested in results than in principle. In economics and politics, as in war, an astonishing number of people die, like the man on the railway crossing, defending their right of way. This is a poorly developed instinct in Switzerland. No country so firmly avows the principles of private enterprise but in few have the practical concessions to socialism been more numerous and varied. When in Switzerland, we bank at a publicly owned cantonal bank, ride the national railroads, pay our bills through the Post Office *giro,* talk on a publicly owned telephone system, send telegrams over state-owned wires, look at public television, get news from the public radio, which can be heard over public telephone wires.

We do not live while there, as do many deserving Swiss, in clean, bright, publicly owned housing, access to which is considered a public right. But we do not pay private insurance on our house because the local government considers it cheaper for the individual and better for the community just to replace a house in case of fire. This is also thought to discourage arson, a risk that is not extreme. Swiss farmers are massively supported by the government, partly because they are thought cheaper for keeping the countryside in condition than a parks service. No industry is so uniquely Swiss as watchmaking. For around half a century the movements of most Swiss watches, a not unimportant feature, have been made by a firm that initially was sponsored by the Swiss government. Only the cases, watchbands, boxes and advertising have their origins in the realm of strict private enterprise. In other countries such arrangements would be thought inconsistent with the fundamental principles of free enterprise. The Swiss do not worry about such trifles.

The Leadership Instinct

The Anglo-American instinct in government is very different from that of the Swiss. We do not solve problems ourselves; we search instead for the man or woman who will do so. Ours is not the politics of people but the politics of leaders. In Switzerland the word leadership is scarcely known. In the United States and Britain it has a familiar and resonant sound.

It's the cause of a wonderful schizophrenia in both British and American political life. All British political journalists of depth deplore the decline of Parliament. American sages weep ecstatically over the congenital ineffectuality of the Congress. People in both countries unite in pleading for better leaders — stronger presidents, the great prime ministers of the past. They are asking for men who would weaken their legislatures yet more.

There could be more power in the democratic process — in the collective judgment of legislators and citizens — than the political sages imagine. That power does not consist primarily in passing or not passing laws. Presidents worry but little about independent legislative action and prime ministers even less. In both countries, and especially in the United States, the legislative power is the power to inform. From this comes the public response, and this response no political leader can ignore. On the Vietnam war, Watergate, the CIA, the international and domestic political legerdemain of the great corporations, the impact of the power to inform was very great in America. A president who wants to act in conflict with the democratic will has only one thought: How can I keep the people on Capitol Hill quiet? Or in ignorance? This would be affirmed if, with help from heaven, one could poll recent presidents on what American political institution they could have best done without. In the unlikely event of honest answers, all would put congressional committees and their investigations either at the top of their list or right next to the press.

I've spent a good part of my adult life writing in Switzerland. A great deal of the rest, I sometimes think, has been spent before congressional committees. I exaggerate only slightly. My first appearance was forty years ago. At an average of three a year since — a few years none, some as many as twenty — that is 120 days, a third of a year. I can look at a committee and, without thought, divide its members into the three basic categories — those members you might persuade; those you watch, for their questions could be mean and even damaging; those you can safely ignore. "Professor, to get down to the practical level: How would this affect the average guy in my part of Michigan?" But there is merit even in the mentally retarded legislator. He asks the questions that everyone is afraid to ask for fear of seeming simple.

The legislative hearing informs. Along with the legislative debate it also converts the good idea into the human right. Democratic power survives in these institutions. Still, it is with leaders that our politics is concerned. In the United States politics means selecting the president.

Politics as a Spectator Sport

This is a process of which I'm also something of a veteran. In my first campaign I worked on speeches for FDR. I campaigned twice with Adlai Stevenson, and then for John F. Kennedy, Lyndon Johnson, Eugene McCarthy, briefly for Hubert Humphrey and for George McGovern. I have had a growing affinity for lost causes. On occasion, no doubt, I contributed the slight added shove which helped ensure the loss.

Presidential selection for the next campaign begins as the last campaign subsides. In its intensive form it lasts a year, costs hundreds of millions of dollars, has many of the aspects of an endurance contest and, on the record, is erratic. Eugene McCarthy observed that, in the first two hundred years, it brought us from George Washington to Richard Nixon, from John Adams to Spiro Agnew, from John Jay to John Mitchell and from Alexander Hamilton to John Connally. He went on to say, "You have to ask yourself how much more of this kind of progress we can stand."

The convention is a precise clue to the major flaw. It's a great spectacle, and politics in the United States has become a spectator sport. Unlike football or hockey, it's an all-season show. Reporters greatly enjoy it, an enjoyment that is enhanced because they can believe, as they cannot of watching a football game, that their work has redeeming social consequence. When, as sometimes happens, they are assailed by doubt, they remind their audience, and therewith themselves, that history is being made. As in football, it is form that counts, not substance. Points are awarded not for wisdom on issues but for performance in the game. Winning is, of course, the only test of achievement.

All this becomes evident at a national convention. It is covered at vast expense by the television networks. Their most experienced commentators patrol the floor. Their experience is with tactics and strategy; they are not expected to feel deeply about issues or policy. In tense, confidential, condescending tones they tell their audience of history in the making. It is a history that all sensible historians will ignore. Reporters interview the managers of the several candidates, the leaders of the state delegations. These tell of complex designs which will soon be abandoned and hopes presented as predictions that will never be fulfilled. Again I speak from some experience. I've been attending these festivals, off and on, since 1940. I was a floor coordinator for Kennedy in 1960, a floor manager for McCarthy in 1968, a McGovern archon in 1972. I've sat through many weary hours as a delegate. My bottom bears a permanent latticework design from the chairs. Once I opposed, and possibly helped to veto, the proposed selection of a vice-president. It was because I was thought to have power in my delegation which I didn't in the slightest possess. There was no chance that its members would necessarily agree with me. With that negative exception, I do not believe that I ever had the slightest influence on the selection of a candidate. Once, in Los Angeles, I did tell Edward R. Murrow, who asked me, that "everything was under control." He went immediately to the booth and reported it to Walter Cronkite. They were both very excited. So, the Kennedy forces were admitting that they had everything under control. They discussed this compelling piece of news for five full minutes.

Once the convention that the commentators believe still to exist did assemble. In the case of the Democrats it was made up of two major groups — semi-literates from the rural South and semi-criminals from the urban North. Both were under the command of those who had selected them. The first were kept in line by playing on their natural awe of their surroundings and the threat of not paying their return fare. Those from Tammany, Jersey City, Boston, Chicago, Kansas City knew they could be deprived of illegal income, even threatened with imprisonment, if they did not conform. These malleable statesmen could, accordingly, be bartered or brokered. They are gone forever. Delegates of intelligence and honesty now assemble with their minds made up. The real decisions on candidates come before, in the primaries and the state caucuses and conventions.

The Equilibrium

Henceforth, when the California primary, the last and the largest, is over, we will almost always know who the candidates will be. This is another giant step toward democracy. The conventions, in their great days, gave power to the few. The primaries give it to the people. As with many others, my commitment to democracy is an article of faith, and I am not really open to argument on the alternatives. But I do think there is rational ground for believing it to be both stronger and safer than any other form. This is because weakness and danger in the modern state come when there is a rift between governing and governed — when people can feel that government is not theirs. The more democratic the process, the less this danger, the smaller this weakness. When people put their ballots in the boxes, they are, by that act, inoculated against the feeling that the government is not theirs. They then accept, in some measure, that its errors are their errors, its aberrations their aberrations, that any revolt will be against themselves. It's a remarkably shrewd and rather conservative arrangement when one thinks of it.

But what we call democracy is considerably less than that. The limousines at the candidates' headquarters on election night are a clue. Our electoral system gives power to the voter. And, let there be no doubt, it gives power to money. The people are many, the rich are few. But politicians need money. And the well-to-do are far more articulate than the average, which is why their indignation is regularly mistaken for the voice of the masses. The result is an equilibrium between voters and money.

But even here democracy is advancing. Public funds now pay a part of the election costs. The rich are not quite as much needed as before.

The Nature of Leadership

For what do people look in leaders, however selected? For what should they look?

Again I plead some qualification. I've had a distant acquaintance with most of the political leaders of the last half century. I missed Hitler, Mussolini and also Stalin. Hermann Goering, Joachim von Ribbentrop, Albert Speer, Walther Funk, Julius Streicher and Robert Ley did pass under my inspection and interrogation in 1945 but they only proved that National Socialism was a gangster interlude at a rather low order of mental capacity and with a surprisingly high incidence of alcoholism.

All of the great leaders have had one characteristic in common: it was the willingness to confront unequivocally the major anxiety of their people in their time. This, and not much else, is the essence of leadership.

In 1933, the Great Depression was the great and pervading source of anxiety. President Hoover was not a foolish man; few have been trained more comprehensively for the presidency. But he could not face directly the economic disaster of his time. Repeatedly he told people who knew better that the slump was over. Roosevelt, in his Inaugural Address and in the legislation of the first hundred days, left no one in doubt. All his energies would be committed to the economic miseries of the time. The people's concern was his concern. What could be done, he would do. There would be no pretense.

Roosevelt was a captivating speaker. He sustained a sense of intimacy with people; he let them believe they were in his confidence. He had charm — it would now for some reason be called charisma. ("Senator Roman Hruska has charisma." "Sir Keith Joseph has charisma.") These qualities would never have been noticed if

Roosevelt had failed to commit himself to the anxieties of the time.

The proof is that these qualities made little impression until he had so committed himself. In 1932, Walter Lippmann looked over the candidates; no one's view was thought to be more acute. Roosevelt, he said, "is a pleasant man, who, without any important qualifications for the office, would very much like to be President."[1] A leader can compromise, get the best bargain he can. Politics is the art of the possible. But he cannot be thought to evade.

Nehru

The leader I knew best was Jawaharlal Nahru. We both had association with the University of Cambridge. Once, when visiting the United States, he expressed amused alarm over the number of Oxford men — William Fulbright, Dean Rusk, numerous others — in high positions. I assured him that, as in India, the decisive posts were held by Cambridge men. He professed great relief.

The issue Nehru confronted, with Gandhi, was the independence of India. India should govern herself. More important was the question of equality and dignity for all the people of India — an end to the belief, accepted as truth for two centuries, that Europeans were superior to Asians. This truth had been proclaimed in the clubs, in the railway stations, on the benches in the parks, in the social life of India.

For Nehru the temptation to equivocate was especially strong. He came from a wealthy, aristocratic, socially conservative family. His father was a pioneer in the Congress Movement but at a time when it met in morning clothes, accepted the Raj and no one needed to be reminded that it had been founded by an Englishman. Nehru himself moved easily among Europeans, often with a poorly concealed sense of his own superior grace and education. Once he told me, again not quite seriously, that he would be the last Englishman to be Prime Minister of India. But he faced the principal issue of his time and accepted fully its personal cost, including the years of imprisonment. This affirmed his right to lead. Had he failed so to commit himself, his charm, his highly informed mind (much more informed than Roosevelt's), his famous sense of community with the Indian masses would have counted for nothing. His name would not now be known.

When Hitler became the great source of anxiety, Roosevelt faced that fear, as did Winston Churchill and Charles de Gaulle. Nehru did not have a similar capacity for change. After independence was won, poverty and the relentless Malthusianism of the Indian people were the all-embracing problems of India. These Nehru did not similarly confront. Surely there was some socialist magic that would wave them away. Heroes of his English years — Sidney and Beatrice Webb, Harold Laski — had thought so, and it must be true. In his last years his leadership suffered. A leader must be able to confront the anxieties of his time. He must also change as these change.

Leadership and Vietnam

John F. Kennedy once told me, as he told others, that he never wanted to let a day go by without asking what he could do to lift the fear of nuclear annihilation from men's minds. If he had lived, it would have been, perhaps, his claim to leadership. We will never know. In his few years he served only to establish a much lesser commitment. That was to the notion that modern government can be interesting, exciting and a proper concern of the idealistic, the enthusiastic and the young.

I came back from India just before Kennedy's death. For much of the rest of the decade I was concerned with what many consider one of the legacies of his presidency, our involvement in Vietnam. I do not share this view; I do know that he was largely responsible for my own education on the subject. Kennedy sent me to Vietnam in the autumn of 1961. A report from Maxwell Taylor and Walt W. Rostow had urged greater involvement, including troops. (They would be disguised, rather imaginatively, as flood control workers.) Kennedy was distressed and guessed I might have a different view. A short passage, helped perhaps by more knowledge and experience of that part of the world than most of my colleagues possessed, persuaded me of the futility and danger of the enterprise. Given the larcenous incompetence and the inspired selfishness and corruption of those with whom we were allied, we could not succeed. There was a more sobering thought: perhaps we should not succeed.

The Vietnam war showed wonderfully the relationship between leadership and commitment. Eugene McCarthy had never previously been celebrated for strong, uncompromising positions. He was amused, civilized and somewhat lazy. It was a time when almost every other major politician was trying to be against the war in principle, for it was a matter of practical necessity. McCarthy scorned such cant and came out in unequivocal opposition. Millions to whom he had previously been unknown flocked to his side.

I had guessed they might. One day in

the late summer of 1967, I went up to Mount Ascutney in Vermont to address a meeting urging the opening of peace negotiations. It was to be held in the ski lodge; a couple of hundred were expected. When we arrived, the mountain top was covered with people. I had a damaging sense of exaltation. A sermon on the mount. People were, indeed, waiting for some leadership, any leadership, on Vietnam. Across the Connecticut River in New Hampshire a few months later, McCarthy came within a few votes of beating Lyndon Johnson in the primary. It was clear that in the Wisconsin primary a few weeks later he would win. Johnson called a halt to the bombing and withdrew as a presidential candidate.

In the next months I marched with Gene, if that is the word, and resisted the thought that Robert Kennedy might be the stronger candidate. Mostly I raised money, an easier thing than might be imagined. People who felt guilty about the war assuaged their conscience with cash. Ours must have been one of the few presidential campaigns in history in which no one worried about finances. I led the McCarthy forces on the convention floor, though without great confidence that I was being followed. I seconded Gene's nomination, and when I returned home, my wife asked what had happened to my speech. The television cameras had all been on the riots downtown. In Chicago I had crossed the police lines to address the more violent protesters. The Chicago police dutifully clubbed others who thought to do so but they recognized a member of the Establishment and escorted me through. It was disconcerting but better than being clubbed.

Of all the men I've known in politics, Eugene McCarthy had the most subtle mind and by far the greatest sense of the music of words. He was, indeed, the first serious poet in the American political pantheon. In speaking for his nomination at Chicago, I said that this might not yet be the age of John Milton but it was no longer the age of John Wayne or John Connally. John Connally was sitting there. New York and California delegates sitting near, with that genius for originality that marks American liberalism, jumped to their feet and proposed sexual violence on Connally. John told reporters, "Where ah come from, it helps to have Galbraith against yoou." We owe the end of the Vietnam war to Eugene McCarthy. If he had not committed himself but had tried like the others to straddle the issue, he too would have remained unknown, with his poetry unheard.

Martin Luther King

One day in the spring of that same year I was to lecture at the University of California at Los Angeles. My lecture was canceled. There was unrest on the campus, and for good reason. Word had come of the killing the day before of Martin Luther King. The Chancellor of UCLA was Franklin Murphy, an old friend. He asked me to speak at a memorial gathering on the campus.

I recalled a meeting with King a year earlier — a long afternoon in Geneva. Andrew Young, now a congressman from Atlanta, was with Dr. King. Like Gandhi and Nehru whom he greatly admired, Martin Luther King had confronted the issue of justice and equality for his people. This he knew to be the only test of a black leader. He knew also, as did Gandhi, that a civilized leader must eschew violence, for violence evokes other anxieties and repels those supporters who are most needed. Now King felt that he must face another issue. Men, black and white, were dying to no purpose in Vietnam. I was identified with that issue, and thus our meeting. He said that a leader must move on to the next great issue when it comes. Some of the lesson that I am stressing here I learned that afternoon.

Berkeley

Is there an education that serves the democratic purpose, gives democracy both power and the wisdom to use it well?

The answer brings me to familiar and beloved scenes, to the older campus of the University of California at Berkeley. I was here during the nineteen-thirties, and we then thought it the best university in the world. I am happy to say that many since have come to accept our insight.

Undergraduates in my day were not politically very concerned; as elsewhere and over the centuries the principal symbols of student achievement were sex, alcohol and idleness, along with a more modern commitment to intercollegiate athletics. But in the sixties Lyndon Johnson, the Vietnam war and the hot breath of the local draft board succeeded where books and professors had failed; the very word Berkeley became a symbol of student involvement in public issues. A massive questioning of the wisdom of accepted authority, many called it a revolt, began here and spread to universities around the world. If you mentioned Berkeley, men and women began to discuss, often with alarm, the role of education in a democracy.

That education has, I believe, two requisites. Both follow directly from the argument I've just made. Education must seek to develop the needed sense of community — the feeling that, at some point, the special interest, even if it is yours, must give way to the general interest; that what best serves all best serves you. With this must go a shrewd awareness that those who resist the general interest must themselves be resisted. When corporations, trade associations, generals, bureaucrats, trade unions, lawyers, physicians, professors put their own pecuniary or bureaucratic interest ahead of the public interest, people must sense, react and oppose. Democratic education must be a lesson in this recognition and this duty.

Second, education must instill the sense of personal security that causes men and women to make a clear and unambiguous commitment to the task at hand, or to distinguish between those who do and those who do not. The evil in modern spectator politics is in the praise it accords the politician who affirms his commitment to the anxieties of the day and then deftly persuades those who dislike the requisite action that they have nothing to fear from his election. "I am for peace but not at the price of weakness." "Poverty must be eliminated but without placing new burdens on the taxpayer." "I stand for a better distribution of income but without interference with the rewards to individual enterprise."

The leaders I have mentioned — Roosevelt, Nehru, Kennedy and, by the standards of his community, Martin Luther King — had what today would be called an elitist education. Perhaps this gave them the sense of security that allowed of their commitment. There is involved here, we should not doubt, a conflict in goals. We want the largest possible number of participants in democratic discussion, and the tens of thousands that the University of California enrolls are proof of the seriousness of the effort. We want these students to believe that, in a democracy, they are sovereign; they have the right and the responsibility and the power to decide. And we want also to train leaders — men and women who are equipped with the knowledge, self-confidence and self-esteem to decide for others and win acceptance for their will. That is the meaning of leadership. We ask, at the same time, for leaders and for followers who are told that leadership belongs to them. It is possible that some conflicts are irreconcilable in principle but not in practice.

Commitment

To understand the importance of commitment is to see in full perspective the problems we have here been discussing. Few, if any, are difficult of solution. The difficulty, all but invariably, is in confronting them. We know what needs to be done; for reasons of inertia, pecuniary interest, passion or ignorance, we do not wish to say so.

The problem of rich countries and poor cannot be solved except by some redistribution of wealth, present or at a minimum potential, between the two groups. That is not difficult to see. But not many want to commit themselves to *that* solution. They are even less inclined to urge what we have seen is the oldest of the remedies, which is for people to move from the poor countries to the rich.

The relentless population increase in the

poor countries cannot be checked except by the control of births. The Chinese, and increasingly the Indians, are concluding that this cannot be purely permissive. Few elsewhere wish to commit themselves to this hard truth.

The poorer the country, the poorer it is in administrative resources — the special case of the Chinese with their ancient organizational skills possibly apart. The less, accordingly, can there be reliance on highly organized effort, of which socialism is the extreme example. The greater the poverty, the more, in general, must the poor countries rely on that release of individual energies that both Adam Smith and Karl Marx believed essential in early economic development. Not many in the poor countries want to confront this seemingly very conservative truth.

In the rich countries there is similar difficulty in confronting the problem of poverty. No solution is so effective as providing income to the poor. Whether in the form of food, housing, health services, education or money, income is an excellent antidote for deprivation. No truth has spawned so much ingenious evasion.

We protect our environment only as we say plainly what can or cannot be done to the ambient air, water, landscape. This is a difficult truth. Better an exception for the energy shortage, to protect jobs, for one's own automobile. We make resources last longer by using less. Also a difficult truth.

No politician can praise unemployment or inflation, and there is no way of combining high employment with stable prices that does not involve some control of income and prices. Otherwise the struggle for more consumption and more income to sustain it — a struggle that modern corporations, modern unions and modern democracy all facilitate and encourage — will drive up prices. Only heavy unemployment will then temper this upward thrust. Not many wish to confront the truth that the modern economy gives a choice only between inflation, unemployment or controls.

The problem of the great metropolis is not complex. Overwhelmingly it is money.

For people to live close by or on top of each other in great numbers is exceedingly expensive. If we so live, we must be prepared to pay. And if people can escape payment by moving from the city, some or many will go. The economic base will then be eroded, the problem of money be more severe. But again it is more blessed to evade. Better a speech promising more efficient city government, a clampdown on wasteful spending, a stronger line with the teachers, the police and the sanitation unions.

Skidoo

The greatest support to evasion comes from complexity. The problem seeming difficult, we postpone, compromise, yield to the conveniences of politics. To see how we use complexity as a device, it is good, on occasion, to go to a community or a countryside where things are sufficiently stark so that evasion is not possible. One admirable such place is Skidoo 23. It is in the Panamint Mountains in California, not far from the Nevada border, 5600 feet over Death Valley. Skidoo is a force for clarity.

It flourished as a mining town in the early part of this century. (The 23 refers, apparently, to the distance water was piped over the mountains to the mines.) Its greatest moment came in 1908, the year of my birth. Skidoo's most dissolute citizen, Joe Simpson, shot and killed Jim Arnold, the storekeeper, banker and the most respected member of the Skidoo Establishment. Simpson was strung up on a telephone pole, the wires of which gave the news to the world. Reporters rushed in, and the media-conscious citizens strung Joe up a second time to show them how justice of a sort had been done.

No one can look at the deserted and empty mine shafts of Skidoo and escape the fact that resources are exhaustible and nonrenewable.

Skidoo shows also how fragile is the fabric of modern urban existence. Once it was a thriving community of 700 souls. Now the population is precisely nil. For Skidoo the problem was the economic base, as no one on this desert could fail to see. When that eroded, so did Skidoo.

Self-interest — the release of individual energies — made Skidoo. No one could imagine that any other force could bring people hundreds and thousands of miles to bury themselves in the holes one sees here. No one here could believe there is some collectivist or socialist miracle that would similarly populate the desert.

In Skidoo men mined gold. Everything there shows finally how much energy men can expend for no social purpose. Let all reflect on the idle piles in which the gold, most of it, still resides. This capacity for wasting effort is a useful thought to take to the subject of competitive weapons manufacture.

Death Valley

Down below Skidoo in Death Valley, truth has also a wonderful clarity of line. Again we see that the problem is in confronting it.

No one is poor in this valley. That is because there is an excellent relationship between land and people. There are no people. If anyone tried to make a living from *this* land, he would not be rich.

On occasion in the past, people have come to the valley. They always moved on. If they could not have done so, they would have been miserable indeed. Such movement from poor lands to rich has been, we've seen, one of the great solvents for poverty, and for a long time. No one here can doubt its need.

I exaggerate slightly. There are a few families in this valley. People live on income that flows in to them from outside. One resident earlier in the century, Death Valley Scotty, was subsidized in much style by an eccentric millionaire and built the castle that still stands. Without such external support, the few people in the valley would starve — or have to go. The situation of the poor countries is the same. For them, too, income from outside is an antidote for poverty. It is no less a remedy for poverty when it comes as aid — a gift. It is a fact which people of the rich countries try very hard to forget.

Death Valley has another and yet more

important truth to affirm. It is 140 miles long, from 4 to 16 miles wide. Imagine it to have been urbanized as the Connecticut-New York-New Jersey-Philadelphia area is urbanized. Or London and the Home Counties. Or the Moscow metropolitan area. Or the Tokyo-Yokohama plain. Imagine that the urban and suburban area covers the whole length and breadth of the valley from the mountains to the mountains. Death Valley is how such a metropolis would look after a mere four twenty-megaton bombs. It is how any metropolitan area of similar extent anywhere in the world would look after a similar weight of bombs. To confront this truth fully we must travel east from Death Valley to the eastern slope of the Rockies to the North American Defense Command — NORAD. It is deep inside Cheyenne Mountain not far from Colorado Springs.

The Nuclear Evasion

The truth that men seek there to evade is that this small planet cannot survive a nuclear exchange; that conflict in support of either national passion or differing ideology is grimly absolute; that those bunkered up within Cheyenne Mountain would last for only a few weeks longer than the possibly more fortunate in the town outside.

We do not yet confront this truth. Asked if we want life for our children and grandchildren, we affirm that we do. Asked about nuclear war, the greatest threat to that life, we regularly dismiss it from mind. Man has learned to live with the thought of his own mortality. And he now has accommodated to the thought that all may die, that his children and grandchildren will not exist. It's a capacity for accommodation at which we can only marvel. I suspect that our minds accept the thought but do not embrace the reality. The act of imagination is too great or too awful. Our minds can extend to a war in some distant jungle and set in motion the actions that reject it. But not yet to the nuclear holocaust.

A commitment to this reality is now the supreme test of our politics. None should accept the easy evasion that the decision is not ours. The Russians are no less perceptive, no less life-enhancing, no more inclined to a death wish than we. Their experience of the death and devastation of war is far more comprehensive than ours. We must believe, for it is true, that they are as willing as we are to commit themselves to this reality, to the existence of this threat to all life and to its elimination.

That, indeed, is the highest purpose of politics in both countries, one that far transcends the differences in economic or political systems. For after the first exchange of missiles, as Khrushchev was moved to warn the world, the ashes of Communism and the ashes of capitalism will be indistinguishable. Not even the most passionate ideologue will be able to speak of the difference, for he too will be dead. In an age when so much is uncertain, there is one certainty: This truth we must confront.

A Major Word of Thanks

These are usually called acknowledgments; for this book it is a grievously inadequate word. Adrian Malone, to whom I have dedicated these pages, was the originator of this enterprise, my companion and mentor throughout. My debt is great to him, and only slightly less to Dick Gilling, Mick Jackson and David Kennard, the three directors who divided and shared responsibility for *The Age of Uncertainty*. Without these four colleagues there would have been no television series and, of course, no book.

Supporting the work of Messrs. Malone, Gilling, Jackson and Kennard and in constant support of me were Sue Burgess, Jenny Doe, Sheila Johns and Sarah Hyde.

These are persons of high proficiency in all the myriad functions that go with filmmaking and its associated and notably proliferated paperwork, and extend on to managing travel, running offices, driving automobiles and typing scripts. This proficiency they combine with great charm and even greater good humor. My thanks to all four are deeply tinged with love.

All who watch television should know — as I now know — that merit depends less on the man on the screen than on the people who put him there. (The man who performs gets the most care and attention, has the best hours and gets the most pay. It is a beautiful arrangement, allowing always for the point of view.) Thus for a year while filming the series, I worked with two superb cameramen, Henry Farrar and Phil Meheux, and Phil, who was longest with us, I shall regard always as one of the most amused, amusing and accomplished artists an economist has ever been privileged to encounter. John Tellick and Dave Brinicombe presided more silently but not less valuably over the sound recording. It is their highly defensible position, rigorously enforced, that, in watching television, people need not only to see clearly but to hear clearly. Robyn Mendelsohn handled all details for the BBC in New York, and in London and on location Kevin Rowley, Jim Black, Kevin Baxendale, Tony Mayne, Dennis Kettle, Dave Gurney, Dave Childs, Terry Manning, Sid Morris, Francis Daniel, Doug Corry, Stuart Moser, Michael Purcilly, Douglas Ernst, John Lindley, Richard Brick, Colin Lowrey, Sue Shearman, Hilary Henson, Barbara Lane, Jacque Jefferies and Jeni Kine assisted on the cameras, on the lights, with the sound, in the studio and even on my face. The list continues: Paul Carter, Jim Latham and Pamela Bosworth were the film editors; Charles McGhie and Karen Godson the graphic designers; John Horton the visual effects designer. On the final programs Peter Bartlett, Elmer Cossey, John Walker and Adam Gifford were the very able cameramen, Chris Cox and Bob McDonnell their assistants.

I must add a special word for Mick Burke who, as assistant cameraman, was a truly good companion through all the early filming. Then he took a leave of absence to join the British team that, in the 1975 season, was to climb Mount Everest. There, a few hundred yards from the top, he walked into the gathering clouds and darkness to complete his passage. He did not return.

Going on from television to this book: Joanna Roll, a family friend, and Ben Shephard of the BBC helped well and diligently on research and checking of facts. Angela Murphy and Paul McAlinden, who also designed the book, searched out and helped select the pictures on these pages.* The arrangement of these illustrations, a thoroughly pleasant chore which I shared, was, like all else, under the direction of Peter Campbell of BBC Publications.

Paul M. Sweezy, an old friend, read the chapter on Marx and gave me much help. Adam Ulam, another friend of distinctly contrasting view, helped me similarly on Lenin. To both, thanks, with full freedom

*Editor's Note: Photographs deleted for Large Print edition of the book.

from responsibility for the result. Among the many others to whom I turned for help, I would like to mention especially Sir Eric Roll, whose eclectic and thoughtful knowledge of the history of economic thought has helped so many of us over the years.

My immediate associates and relatives in Cambridge remain for my final word of thanks. Londa Schiebinger typed and retyped and then went on faithfully to check and correct my facts. Emmy Davis managed the office and much of my life while the enterprise was in progress, in her spare time also typed and checked, and she journeyed with me during the American filming to provide help, protection and safe movement and to calm the emotions of all concerned. As so often before, Andrea Williams was not my assistant but my full-fledged partner. She worked with the BBC on all the details of the television programs, edited this book, saw it through the press, did everything else I would otherwise have had to do.

I've always been suspicious of authors who use these acknowledgments to proclaim their love for their wives. Most likely it is a cover for secret distaste, occasional beatings and adulterous yearnings, fulfilled or unfulfilled. But there are exceptions to the best rules. Catherine Galbraith joined in on this effort from the first day, accompanied me for all the filming, stood off curious intruders by day and by night, showed herself a competent photographer as these pages attest,* performed in the last two programs and kept a journal which will one day tell of the talented people and the improbable procedures with which the BBC produces a television series.

John Kenneth Galbraith
Cambridge, Massachusetts 1976

*Editor's Note: Photographs deleted for Large Print edition of the book.

Notes

Chapter 1

[1] John Maynard Keynes, *The General Theory of Employment Interest and Money* (New York: Harcourt, Brace and Co., 1936), p. 383.

[2] Ibid.

[3] Ibid.

[4] A strong case will be made for F. Y. Edgeworth who, though he spent his life in England, was one of the Edgeworths of Edgeworthstown, County Longford.

[5] Unlike Hume and other men of liberal mind at the time, Adam Smith did not welcome American independence. His vision was of a commonwealth embracing all the English-speaking world. Members from North America would sit in the House of Commons in London; eventually, with increasing population in America, the capital would be moved to a more central location across the Atlantic. Cincinnati, Memphis or, considering the claims of Canada, perhaps Green Bay, Wisconsin. That was the destiny that was missed.

[6]Adam Smith, *Wealth of Nations,* Vol. I (London: Methuen & Co., 1950), p. 412.

[7]Smith, Vol. I, p. 8.

[8]Ibid.

[9]Smith, Vol. I, p. 144.

[10]Smith, Vol. II, p. 264.

[11]Smith, Vol. II, pp. 264 - 265.

[12]William Pitt before the House of Commons on February 17, 1792, quoted in John Rae, *Life of Adam Smith* (New York: Augustus M. Kelley, 1965), pp. 290 - 291.

[13]Charles Edward Trevelyan quoted in Dudley Edwards, *The Great Famine* (Dublin: Brown and Nolan, 1956), p. 257.

Chapter 2

[1]Allan Nevins, *Study in Power,* Vol. II (New York: Charles Scribner's Sons, 1953), p. 300.

[2]Peter Collier and David Horowitz, *The Rockefellers: An American Dynasty* (New York: Holt, Rinehart and Winston, 1976), p. 59. From the manuscript of Frederick T. Gates's unpublished autobiography.

[3]Herbert Spencer, *The Study of Sociology* (New York: D. Appleton and Co., 1891), p. 438.

[4]Herbert Spencer, *Social Statics* (New York: D. Appleton and Co., 1865), p. 413.

[5]William Graham Sumner quoted in Richard Hofstadter, *Social Darwinism in American Thought 1860 - 1915* (Philadelphia: University of Pennsylvania Press, 1945), p. 44.

[6]John D. Rockefeller quoted in Hofstadter, p. 31.

[7]Ibid.

[8]*New York Post,* September 13, 1975.
[9]Henry Ward Beecher quoted in Hofstadter, p. 18.
[10]Thorstein Veblen, *The Theory of the Leisure Class* (Boston: Houghton Mifflin Co., 1973), p. 176.
[11]Veblen, p. 57.
[12]Veblen, p. 64.
[13]Veblen, p. 62.
[14]Veblen, p. 65.
[15]James Gordon Bennett, Sr., quoted in Richard O'Connor, *The* Scandalous *Mr. Bennett* (Garden City, New York: Doubleday & Co., 1962), p. 82.
[16]James Gordon Bennett, Sr., in the *New York Herald,* May 6, 1835, quoted in Don C. Seitz, *The James Gordon Bennetts: Father and Son* (Indianapolis: The Bobbs-Merrill Co., 1928), p. 39.
[17]Gustavus Myers in Matthew Josephson, *The Robber Barons* (New York: Harcourt, Brace and Co., 1934), p. 340.

Chapter 3

[1]Joseph Schumpeter, *Capitalism, Socialism, Democracy,* 3rd ed. (New York: Harper's Torchbooks, 1967), p. 21.
[2]Karl Marx in Karl Marx and Friedrich Engels, *Selected Works,* Vol. II (Moscow: 1962), p. 22.
[3]Karl Marx quoted in David McLellan, *Karl Marx: His Life and Thought* (New York: Harper & Row, 1973), p. 14.
[4]McLellan, p. 16.
[5]Friedrich Engels quoted in McLellan, p. 28.
[6]Karl Marx quoted in McLellan, p. 58.
[7]McLellan, pp. 56 - 57.

[8]Karl Marx quoted in McLellan, p. 56.

[9]Karl Marx quoted in McLellan, p. 60.

[10]*Karl Marx: Early Texts,* David McLellan, ed. (Oxford: Blackwell, 1972), p. 129.

[11]Friedrich Engels quoted in McLellan, p. 131.

[12]Karl Marx in Karl Marx and Friedrich Engels, Vol. I, p. 52.

[13]Eric Roll, *A History of Economic Thought* (London: Faber & Faber, 1973), pp. 257 - 258.

[14]*Karl Marx: Early Texts,* p. 217.

[15]Karl Marx, *The Communist Manifesto,* in Karl Marx and Friedrich Engels, Vol. I, pp. 108 - 137.

[16]Karl Marx, *The Communist Manifesto,* in Karl Marx and Friedrich Engels, Vol. I, p. 126.

[17]Karl Marx, *The Revolutions of 1848,* Vol. I: Political Writings. (London: Allen Lane and New Left Review, 1973), p. 129.

[18]A spy for the Prussian government quoted in McLellan, pp. 268 - 269.

[19]Jenny Marx quoted in McLellan, p. 265.

[20]Sir George Grey, British Home Secretary, quoted in McLellan, p. 231.

[21]Karl Marx, *Capital: a Critique of Political Economy,* Vol. I (Chicago: Charles H. Kerr & Co., 1926), pp. 836 - 837.

[22]Karl Marx quoted in McLellan, p. 315.

[23]Karl Marx, *The Civil War in France: Address of the International Working Men's Association,* quoted in Karl Marx and Friedrich Engels, Vol. II, p. 208.

[24]Karl Marx, *Address to the Working Classes,* quoted in McLellan, pp. 365 - 366.

[25]Karl Marx, *The Civil War in France,* quoted in McLellan, p. 400.

[26]Karl Marx, *Critique of the Gotha Programme,* quoted in McLellan, p. 433.

Chapter 4

[1]Adam Smith, *Wealth of Nations,* Vol. II (London: Methuen & Co., 1950), p. 158.

[2]Smith, Vol. II, p. 131.

[3]James Mill quoted in "Biographical Sketch" by Donald Winch in *James Mill, Selected Economic Writings,* Donald Winch, ed. (Edinburgh & London: Oliver & Boyd, 1966), p. 19.

[4]R. Ewart Oakeshott, *The Archaeology of Weapons* (London: Lutterworth Press, 1960), p. 183.

[5]Pope Innocent III quoted in Henry Treece, *The Crusades* (New York: Random House, 1963), p. 229.

[6]Smith, Vol. II, p. 72.

[7]William Hickling Prescott, *History of the Conquest of Mexico,* Vol. I (New York: John B. Alden, 1886), p. 163.

[8]Prescott, pp. 163 - 164.

[9]Prescott, p. 165.

[10]William Hickling Prescott, *History of the Conquest of Peru* (London: Richard Bentley, 1854), p. 314.

[11]See Chapter VI, pp. 170 - 174.

[12]*Letters of Marie-Madeleine Hachard, Ursuline of New Orleans 1727 - 1728* (New Orleans: Laboard Printing Co., 1974), p. 58.

[13]John Beames, *Memoirs of a Bengal Civilian* (London: Chatto & Windus, 1961).

[14]Beames, p. 151.

[15]Rudyard Kipling, *A Choice of Kipling's Verses Made by T. S. Eliot* (New York: Charles Scribner's

Sons, 1943), pp. 136 - 137.

Chapter 5

[1]Hugo Gaase quoted in *Verhandlungen des Reichstags,* Stenographische Berichte, Band 306 (Berlin: Norddeutschen Buchdruckerei und Verlags-Anstalt, 1916), p. 9.

[2]*Fireside Book of Humorous Poetry,* William Cole, ed. (New York: Simon and Schuster, 1959), p. 122.

[3]V. I. Lenin quoted in N. K. Krupskaya, *Reminiscences of Lenin* (Moscow: Foreign Languages Publishing House, 1959), p. 258.

[4]N. K. Krupskaya, p. 307.

[5]V. I. Lenin, *Imperialism: the Highest Stage of Capitalism* (Moscow: Foreign Languages Publishing House, 1947), p. 16.

[6]V. I. Lenin quoted in N. K. Krupskaya, p. 323.

[7]V. I. Lenin quoted in N. K. Krupskaya, p. 335.

[8]Christopher Hill, *Lenin and the Russian Revolution* (London: The English Universities Press, 1947), p. 117.

[9]V. I. Lenin, *The State and Revolution* (Moscow: Progress Publishers, 1969), p. 92.

[10]V. I. Lenin quoted in Hill, pp. 208 - 209.

[11]Adam Ulam, *The Bolsheviks* (New York: The Macmillan Co., 1965), p. 531.

Chapter 6

[1]Herodotus, Book I, *Clio,* Rev. William Beloe, trans. (Philadelphia: M'Carty and Davis, 1844), p. 31.

[2]Charles Mackay, *Memoirs of Extraordinary Popular*

Delusions and the Madness of Crowds (Boston: L. C. Page and Co., 1932), p. 55.

[3] A. Andreades, *History of the Bank of England* (London: P. S. King and Son, 1909), p. 250, citing Juglar, *Les Crises Economiques,* p. 334.

[4] Nicholas Biddle quoted in Arthur M. Schlesinger, Jr., *The Age of Jackson* (Boston: Little, Brown & Co., 1946), p. 75.

[5] Andrew Jackson quoted in J. D. Richardson, *A Compilation of the Messages and Papers of the Presidents 1789 - 1908,* Vol II (Washington: Bureau of National Literature and Art, 1908), p. 581.

Chapter 7

[1] John Maynard Keynes, *My Early Beliefs* in *Two Memoirs* (London: Rupert Hart-Davis, 1949), p. 83.

[2] John Maynard Keynes quoted in R. F. Harrod, *The Life of John Maynard Keynes* (London: Macmillan & Co., 1951), p. 121.

[3] John Maynard Keynes, *Essays in Biography* (London: Mercury Books, 1961), p. 20.

[4] John Maynard Keynes quoted in Harrod, p. 257.

[5] John Maynard Keynes quoted in Harrod, p. 256.

[6] Robert Lekachman, *Keynes' General Theory: Reports of Three Decades* (New York: St. Martin's Press, 1964), p. 35.

[7] John Maynard Keynes, *Essays in Persuasion* (London: Macmillan & Co., 1931), pp. 248 - 249.

[8] John Maynard Keynes quoted in Robert Lekachman, *The Age of Keynes* (New York: Random House, 1966), p. 47.

[9] Herbert Hoover quoted in Arthur M. Schlesinger, Jr.,

The Crisis of the Old Order (Boston: Houghton Mifflin Co., 1957), p. 231.

[10]John Maynard Keynes quoted in Harrod, p. 447.

[11]Franklin D. Roosevelt quoted in Lekachman, *The Age of Keynes,* p. 123.

[12]John Maynard Keynes quoted in Lekachman, *The Age of Keynes,* p. 123.

[13]John Maynard Keynes quoted in Harrod, p. 462.

Chapter 8

[1]Adlai Stevenson quoted in John Bartlow Martin, *Adlai Stevenson of Illinois* (New York: Doubleday & Co., 1976), p. 743.

[2]Townsend Hoopes, *The Devil and John Foster Dulles* (Boston and Toronto: Atlantic Monthly Press Book, Little, Brown and Co., 1973), p. 426.

[3]Reinhold Niebuhr quoted in Hoopes, p. 37.

[4]John Foster Dulles, "Faith of Our Fathers," based on an address given at the First Presbyterian Church of Watertown, New York. U.S. Department of State publication 5300, General Foreign Policy Series 84, released January 1954, pp. 5 - 6.

[5]Dulles, p. 6.

[6]John Foster Dulles, "Freedom and Its Purpose," *The Christian Century* (December 24, 1952), p. 1496.

Chapter 9

[1]Paul A. Samuelson, *Economics,* 9th ed. (New York: McGraw-Hill, 1973), p. 58. The same point, in slightly different words, is made in earlier editions.

[2]Paul A. Samuelson quoted in *Newsweek,*

September 8, 1975, p. 62.

Chapter 10

[1]These figures are derived from "Area and Production of Principal Crops," 1960/61 and 1973/74 issues and preliminary reports from Ministry of Agriculture, New Delhi, and IN 6005, 1 - 21 - 76, from the U.S. Agricultural Attache in New Delhi.

[2]Robert William Fogel and Stanley L. Engerman, *Time on the Cross* (Boston: Little, Brown and Co., 1974).

[3]These figures are derived from U.S. Bureau of the Census, Sixteenth Census of the United States: 1940 Population, Vol. II, *Characteristics of the Population* (Washington, D.C.: U.S. Government Printing Office, 1943) and U.S. Bureau of the Census, Census of the Population: 1970, Vol. I, *Characteristics of the Population* (Washington, D.C.: U.S. Government Printing Office, 1973).

[4]Henry Bamford Parkes, *A History of Mexico*, Sentry ed. (Boston: Houghton Mifflin Co., 1969), pp. 305 - 306.

[5]Colonel Thomas Talbot quoted in Fred Coyne Hamil, *Lake Erie Baron* (Toronto: The Macmillan Co. of Canada, 1955), p. 146.

Chapter 11

[1]Figures for the United States, Britain, Italy and India are from *The Yearbook of Labour Statistics* (Geneva: International Labour Office, 1975).

[2]Bamber Gascoigne, *The Great Moghuls* (New York:

Harper & Row, 1971), p. 95.

[3]Viscount James Bryce, *The American Commonwealth,* 3rd ed., Vol. I (New York: Macmillan and Co., 1893), p. 637.

[4]Paul Mantoux, *The Industrial Revolution in the Eighteenth Century,* rev. ed. (London: Jonathan Cape, 1961), p. 182.

[5]Ibid.

Chapter 12

[1]Arthur M. Schlesinger, Jr., *The Crisis of the Old Order* (Boston: Houghton Mifflin Co., 1957), p. 291.

Index

Acheson, Dean, 422

Acre: assault on (1291), 195

Adams, Henry, 85

Addams, Charles, 456

Address to the Working Classes (Marx), 174

affluent class: display of, 94 - 102; enjoyments, 99 - 101, 103 - 110; God and, 83 - 87; natural selection of, 64 - 74, 75; publicity, 101 - 102; of today, 110 - 117; Veblen on, 87 - 99

agriculture: collectivization, 271, 363; economy of, before Industrial Revolution, 13 - 16; in eighteenth-century France, 22 - 25; Soviet shortcomings, 271, 272, 363

Airey, Colonel Richard, 527

Akbar the Great, 541, 542

Alaska, 212

Algeria, 223

Alsace-Lorraine, 231, 235

America — *see* United States

American Civil War: financed by paper money, 313, 314, 322; as revolt against colonial society, 212, 213

American Dilemma, An (Myrdal), 509

Amsterdam: banks and creation of money, 288 - 294

Armand, Inessa, 268

armed services, and close relationship with industry, 399, 407, 422, 423, 431, 445 - 448

arms race, 397 - 400, 442 - 448

Arnold, Jim (Skidoo storekeeper), 613

Austria, pre-1914 alliance with Germany, 232, 233

automobile industry, Italian and Soviet, 273

Ball, George, 402, 403, 437

Bangladesh: equilibrium of poverty, 37, 502, 503; famine, 51, 52

Bank of Amsterdam, 292 - 294

Bank of England: founding of, 301; Court of Directors, 302; and control of creation of money, 302 - 305, 317; and lending to clearing banks, 305, 306, 325; capacity for economic innovation, 307

Bank for International Reconstruction and Development, 389, 390

Bank Rate, 305, 308, 325

banks and banking, 287 - 308, 315 - 322, 326 - 332; Amsterdam and, 288 - 294; central banks, 306, 315 - 318, 329 - 332; creation of money, 287 - 294, 303; Depression, 330 - 332; failures, 327, 328; regulation of money, 289 - 290, 301, 304 - 305

Banque Royale, 295 - 299

Barnard, George Gardner, 78 - 79

Bay of Pigs (1961), 432 - 435

Beames, John: his ideal of government, 215 - 216

Beecher, Rev. Henry Ward, 125; and Spencer and natural selection, 73, 85, 86

Ben Bella, Ahmed, 223

Bennett, James Gordon, 102, 320

Bennett, James Gordon, Jr., 102, 106

Berkeley, University of California at, 343, 605 - 608
Berle, Adolf A., 471
Berlin: Marx and, 127 - 133; Wall, 132, 133;
    Brandenburg Gate, 404; airlift, 409 - 410; post-war,
    400 - 410
Bern, Lenin in, 252, 256
Biddle, Nicholas: showdown with Andrew Jackson
    over bank power, 320
Birmingham (Alabama), 553 - 554
Birmingham (England), 553
Birmingham (Michigan), 561
birth control, 59, 506 - 510, 609, 610
Bismarck, Otto von, 175, 176
Blaine, James G., 383
Blanc, Louis, 143, 154
Blanqui, Louis Auguste, 143
Blenheim Palace, 107
Bloomsbury Group, 342
Blue Ridge Corporation, 358, 416
Bolsheviks, 241. *See also* Communism
Bonn University, Marx at, 127
Brattleboro (Vermont), Kipling at, 219, 225
"Breakers, The" (Vanderbilt mansion, Newport), 97
Bretton Woods Conference (1944), 389
Britain: landowners and workers' rights, 15; loss of
    American colonies, 49; expansion of production and
    trade, 49; and colonialism, 214, 215; pre-1914 trade
    unions, 228; and World War I, 241, 260, 261; ruling
    coalition of capitalists and workers, 276, 277;
    banking system, 301 - 308, 315 - 317, 325; return to
    gold standard, 349 - 354; unemployment, 352, 353;
    Great Depression, 365; economic policy during
    World War II, 387; and immigration, 522, 562, 563,

637

565, 566; low productivity of labor force, 522, 523;
  agricultural labor force, 537; race prejudice, 565
British Museum Reading Room, 253; Marx and, 167;
  Lenin and, 253
Brooklyn, Plymouth Church, 84
Bruges: as Merchant City, 546, 547
Brüning, Heinrich, 364
Brussels, 469; Marx in, 147, 161
Bryan, William Jennings, 84, 318; opposes gold
  standard, 324
Bryce, Lord, 557
Bryce, Robert, 374, 375
Burke, Admiral Arleigh, 444

California: emigration of poor whites into, 567 - 568;
  University of, Berkeley, 605 - 608
Callaghan, James, 17
Calvin, John, 581
Camp city, 558 - 561
Canada: and World War I, 260, 264, 279; quiet
  revolution, 278; and variant of paper money, 310 -
  312; and Keynesian doctrine, 375; settling of West,
  529, 530
Cap Ferrat, 106
capitalism: coalition with workers after World War I,
  276, 277; converging with Communism in business,
  272, 273; Marx's theory of, 167 - 171; motivating
  influence in change, 145; overthrow of, by
  proletariat, 130, 170, 171, 257
capitalism: manners and morals of, 61 - 117;
  ceremonials, 99 - 101; Conspicuous Consumption
  and Leisure, 93 - 110; gambling, 108 - 110; modern
  rich, 110 - 117; natural selection of affluent, 64 - 74;

natural selection and the Church, 83 - 87; railroad struggle, 75 - 83; publicity, 101, 102; Riviera, 103 - 108; Veblen on, 87 - 99

Carey, Henry Charles, challenges Ricardo's view, 57

Carnegie, Andrew, 61

Castellane, Count Boni de, 108

Castro, Fidel, 208

Central Intelligence Agency (CIA): and Cold War, 424 - 426, 432 - 435; in India, 426 - 427*n;* and Bay of Pigs, 432 - 434

Chamberlain, Houston Stewart, 10

Chamberlain, Joseph, 553

Chase Manhattan Bank, 312

Cheyenne Mountain (Colorado), 616, 617

Chiang Kai-shek, 439

Chicago Convention (1968), 603

China, 439, 440; Revolution after World War II, 157, 410; and coinage, 284; enmity with Soviets, 223, 441, 442; birth control, 509, 510, 610

Cholera Bay (Quebec), 55

Churchill family, 107

Churchill, Lord Randolph, 108

Churchill, Lady Randolph, 108

Churchill, Winston, 108, 251, 341, 389, 417; disastrous return to gold standard, 349 - 352, 360, 361; and General Strike, 353, 354

city life: Camp, 558 - 561; Industrial City, 549 - 565; Merchant City, 545 - 548; Metropolis, 566 - 576; migration, 561 - 565; Political Household, 539 - 544, 550, 573, 574; race prejudice, 567

city state, 531 - 536

Civil War in France, The (Marx), 179

class structure, ungluing of in World War I, 227 - 229

Clay, Henry, 320
Clay, General Lucius, 409
Clearances, the, 33 - 37, 512, 561
Clemenceau, Georges: Keynes on, 345
coinage; debasing of, 289; invention of, 284, 308
Cold War, 411, 413, 414, 427 - 442; moral sanction
   for, 414, 415, 418 - 420, 421, 434, 435, 438 - 440
Cologne, Marx's journalism in, 134 - 138
colonialism, 183 - 225; Britain and, 214 - 218; as
   Crusades in Eastern Mediterranean, 192 - 198;
   Eastern European form of, 230 - 232; fiscal aspect,
   196 - 198; France and, 210 - 212, 296, 297; ideas
   governing, 188 - 192; Marx on, 187, 188, 257 - 259;
   revolts against, 208, 212, 213; Adam Smith on, 184,
   185, 200; Spain and, 198 - 208; United States and,
   209, 218 - 222
Columbus, Christopher: and colonialism, 199, 204
commitment, 609 - 612
Committee for Economic Development, 388
Communism, Communists: American aim to save
   Vietnam from, 221; and Cold War, 412, 413, 418,
   419, 427 - 442; converging with capitalism in
   business, 273; divisions within, 428 - 432, 441, 442;
   Lenin's insistence on term, 247; victory in Eastern
   Europe and Asia, 410, 411; Vietnam war's effect on,
   440 - 442
Communist League, 147, 166
Communist Manifesto, The (Marx), 147 - 153
Company of the West (Mississippi Company), rise and
   fall of, 296 - 300
Connally, John, 603, 604
Conspicuous Consumption, 93 - 110
Conspicuous Leisure, 95

Constantinople, 194

Continental Congress, and paper money, 313, 314, 335

corporations, 451 - 498; control of, 471 - 473; Esalen Institute, 455 - 459; future of, 491 - 498; multinational syndrome, 487 - 491; myth of, 451 - 455, 476, 486, 487; Philips, 478 - 486; power of, 452 - 455; Adam Smith on, 31 - 33, 44, 578; UGE, 459 - 478; unease over, 455, 485 - 487

Cortés, Hernando, 204

cotton economy, 512 - 518

Cracow, 230, 231; Lenin in, 230, 242 - 243

Critique of the Gotha Programme (Marx), 180

Cronkite, Walter, 592

Crosby, James S., 444

Crossman, Richard, 35

Crusades: as colonial enterprise, 192 - 198, 203, 204; myth of, 193, 194

Cuba, 432 - 435; break with colonialism, 208; missile crisis, 435 - 437

Currie, General Sir Arthur W., 279

Currie, Lauchlin, 382; as exponent of Keynes in Washington, 378 - 380

Czechoslovakia, Soviet takeover, 410, 411

Dale, David: New Lanark experiment, 38

Dallas (Texas), Conspicuous Consumption in, 113

Darien venture, 302

Dark Thursday (1929), 359 - 362

Darrow, Clarence, 84

Darwin, Charles, 65; Spencer's debt to, 66; and natural selection, 83 - 85

Davies-Monthan Air Force Base, 446, 450

Dead Souls (Gogol), 115

Death Valley (California), 614 - 616
democracy: commitment, 609 - 612; education in, 605 - 609; elections, 589 - 595; leadership, 586 - 589, 595 - 605; Swiss model, 580 - 586
Democratic Advisory Council, 422
Detroit, 531
Dewey, Thomas E., 46
Dominicans, and Spanish colonialism, 201
Drew, Daniel: and Erie Railroad, 77 - 79
Dulles, Allen Welsh, 415; and CIA, 425, 426, 432, 435
Dulles, John Foster, 359, 412 - 421; moral sanction for Cold War, 414, 415, 418 - 422, 432, 438; career, 415 - 418
Dutch East India Company, 293

Eastern Europe, pre-1914 aristocratic ruling class, 227, 228; and revolution, 289; rule of Europeans by other Europeans, 230 - 232; retreat from imperialism, 232; and World War I, 234 - 241; Soviet consolidation in, 405; emigration to industrialized countries, 521, 522, 562
Eastern Mediterranean, Crusades as colonial enterprise in, 192 - 198
East India Company: as source of income for economists, 43, 186; condemned by Adam Smith, 184, 185; and colonialism, 185, 186, 214, 215
Ebert, Friedrich, 275
Eccles, Marriner, 378, 379
Economic Consequences of the Peace, The (Keynes), 346, 389
education, role in democracy, 605 - 609
Edward VII, 319
Eindhoven, as Philips headquarters, 478 - 485

Eisenhower, Dwight D., 411, 434; on danger of misplaced military-industrial power, 396, 398, 431

emigration, 55 - 57, 511 - 531, 561 - 568

Engels, Friedrich, 181; on Hegel, 129; as Marx's partner, 141, 142, 147, 162, 172

England — *see* Britain

Equity Funding Corporation, 116

Erie Railroad war, 76 - 80

Esalen Institute, 455 - 457

Essay on the Principle of Population (Malthus), 185

European Common Market, 490

famine, 44, 52 - 54

Farm Bureau Federation, 23

Fatehpur Sikri: as archetype of Political Household, 540 - 544

Federal Reserve System, 329 - 332; and Keynesian Revolution, 379

Feuerbach, Ludwig, 143

Filene, Edward A., 243

Financial and Industrial Securities Corporation, 358

First Bank of the United States, 318

First International: founding of, 173 - 175; death of, 176; Marx's final address to, 179

Fish, Mrs. Stuyvesant, 100; party given by, 100, 101

Fisher, Irving: formula to determine value of money, 334 - 338, 365; influence on Keynes, 338

Fisk, Jim: and struggle for Erie Railroad, 77 - 80

Ford, Gerald, and détente, 442

Fourier, Charles, 143, 154

France: land-ownership before Industrial Revolution, 15; Adam Smith's impression of, 22, 23; agricultural system, 22, 23; Physiocrats, 23, 24, 26; 1848

Revolution, 152 - 160; 1871 Commune, 177 - 179;
and colonialism, 210 - 212, 296 - 298; pre-1914
workers' political strength, 228, 229; pre-1914
alliance with Russia, 233; and territorial imperative,
235; and World War I, 240, 247, 261; ruling coalition
of capitalists and workers, 276; finances under Law,
295 - 300; Revolution financed by paper money, 313
Franco-Prussian War, 177
Franklin, Benjamin, 20; exponent of paper money,
309, 310, 314
Franklin National Bank, 293
Funk, Walther, 595

Gandhi, Mahatma, 598, 604, 605
Gary, Elbert Henry, 554
Gates, Frederick T., 61, 62
Gaulle, Charles de, 417, 599
General Motors, 492, 493
General Strike (1926), 353, 354
*General Theory of Employment Interest and Money,
The* (Keynes), 370 - 374, 376
George, Henry, *Progress and Poverty,* 93
German-French Yearbooks, Marx's editorship of, 139 -
141
Germany: workers' political strength after 1870, 180,
228, 229; pre-1914 imperialism, 231; and territorial
imperative, 234 - 236; and World War I, 239, 240,
247, 261, 262, 274, 275; fascism, 277, 367; inflation,
328; reparations, 345; Great Depression, 364; Nazi
borrowing and spending to cure unemployment, 366,
367, 381; and Marshall aid, 391
Getting, Ivan, 444
Gide, André, 139

Glow, Arthur Francis, 464
Glow, James B: and founding of UGE, 459 - 462
Glow, James B., Jr., 462 - 465, 471, 474
Goebbels, Joseph, 9
Gogol, Nikolai, *Dead Souls,* 115
Goldblum, Stanley, 115
Goldman Sachs Trading Corporation, 357 - 359
gold standard, 323 - 326, 329; Britain's return to, 349 -
    354; abandonment of, 365
Goodhart, Arthur L., 128
Gotha, working-class parties' program, 180
Gould, Anna, 108
Gould, Jay: and Erie Railroad, 77, 79
Great Crash (1929), 330, 362
Great Depression, 327 - 332, 362 - 365, 596; Keynes's
    remedy for, 365 - 395
Great Hunger, 52 - 53, 57, 58, 186
Greenbacks, 315, 323, 324, 335
Griffin, James (Erie engine driver) 81
Grosse Isle (Quebec), 55

Haase, Hugo, 239
Hachard, Marie-Madeleine, 211
Hamilton, Alexander, 318
Hansen, Alvin Harvey, as American exponent of
    Keynes, 380
Harris, Seymour F., 380
Harvard Business School, 481
Harvard University, Keynes's influence on, 373 - 375
Haughton, Daniel J., on "kickbacks" in arms race,
    397, 399
Hegel, Georg Wilhelm Friedrich, 128 - 131; Marx's
    acceptance of, 129 - 133

Herodotus, on invention of coined money, 284
Highgate Cemetery, Marx's grave, 119
History of British India (Mill), 186
History of the Conquest of Mexico (Prescott), 201
History of the Conquest of Peru (Prescott), 201, 205
Hitler, Adolf, 9, 124; economic policy, 366 - 368, 381;
  as true protagonist of Keynesian ideas, 381
Hobson, J. A., 257
Hofstadter, Richard, 72
Hoover, Herbert: and Great Depression, 362, 364, 596
Hughes, Howard, 101
Hume, David, 19, 34
Humphrey, Hubert, 587
Hungary, revolt (1956), 421

imperialism — *see* colonialism
Imperialism: the Highest Stage of Capitalism (Lenin),
  256, 257
India: land-ownership by Moghuls, 15, 16; equilibrium
  of poverty, 37, 503 - 506; famine, 51, 52; colonialism
  in, 185, 186, 214 - 218; result of independence, 218,
  599; American aid, 225; CIA in, 426 - 427*n*;
  agricultural labor force, 537
Indonesia, and equilibrium of poverty, 37
Industrial City, 549 - 565; as characteristic city, 549 -
  552; class structure, 558 - 560; economics of, 556 -
  558; migration to, 561 - 568; suburb, 559 - 561
Industrial Revolution, 13, 15, 34, 512, 549
Indus Valley, and coinage, 284
inevitable conflict, doctrine of, 398, 408, 421 - 432;
  440, abandonment of, 442
inflation: Germany, 328; Keynes's remedy, 382 - 387,
  393 - 395, 533

Innocent III, Pope, 194

INSEAD (French business school), 481

International Monetary Fund, 390

Ireland: Malthus and Ricardo ideas tested in Great Hunger, 50 - 54; emigrants to America, 55 - 58; 186; 562

Iselin, Columbus, 44

Italy: automobile industry, 272, 273; famine, 274; agricultural labor force, 537

Jackson, Andrew, and struggle against Biddle's bank, 318 - 320

Jefferson, Thomas, 212

Jerusalem, and Crusades, 193, 194, 221

Johnson, Lyndon, 589, 602

Johnson, Dr. Samuel, on London, 549

Jones, Lewis, 427*n*

Jordan, David Starr, 92

Kapital, Das (Marx), 167 - 172

Kapitza, Peter, 273

Kennedy, John F., 96, 427*n*, 589, 591, 592, 608; and Cuban missile crisis, 437; as a leader, 600, 601

Kennedy, Robert, 437, 602

Keynes, Florence Ada, 340

Keynes, John Maynard, 23, 447, 533; on power of vested interests compared with encroachment of ideas, 9, 10; and shortage of purchasing power, 49; on ideas as motivating force in change, 58, 143; his debt to Irving Fisher, 338, 365; at Cambridge, 340 - 343; interest in economics, 342; at Treasury during World War I, 344 - 345; condemns reparations in *Economic Consequences of the Peace*, 346, 389;

unpopularity, 347, 354; attacks return to gold standard, 352 - 354, 389; advocates government borrowing and spending as cure for Depression, 365 - 368; his *General Theory of Employment Interest and Money,* 370 - 372, 376; his views in America and Canada, 373 - 381, 387 - 391, 392 - 395; his cure for inflation, 382 - 387, 394; at Bretton Woods, 389 - 391; negotiates American loan, 390; "legacy" of, 391 - 395

Keynes, John Neville, 341

Khrushchev, Nikita, 271, 618; as decisive man of midcentury, 427 - 432; reverses Stalinist policies, 429, 430; and peaceful coexistence, 429

Kienthal, socialists' conference (1916), 259

King, Martin Luther, 608, and leadership, 604 - 605

Kipling, Rudyard, 219

Kirkcaldy, birthplace of Adam Smith, 17

Knights of the Hospital of St. John of Jerusalem, 196 - 197

Korea, 411

Krak des Chevaliers, 197

Krueznach, 138

Krupskaya, Nedezhda, 242, 253, 266

labor, division of, 28 - 31

labor theory of value, 42, 46, 50, 51, 168

Lahore, 213

landlords: absentee Irish, 51; Malthus and Ricardo theories on revenue of, 47, 48; power of, against workers, 14, 46, 47

Lassalle, Ferdinand, 143

Latin America, colonialism and, 199 - 209

Law, John, 210; and Banque Royale, 295 - 300; and

Mississippi Company, 296 - 300; collapse of schemes, 299, 300

leadership instinct, 586 - 589, 595 - 605

League of the Just (later Communist League), 147

Lenin, V. I., 363; in Cracow, 230, 242 - 243; as true revolutionary compared with Marx, 242 - 246; on role of peasants in revolution, 247 - 249, in Switzerland, 249, 252 - 259, 265, 266; revolutionary conferences, 254 - 256, 259, 260; theory of imperialism and capitalism, 256 - 259; and 1917 Revolution, 265 - 270; takes power in Petrograd, 268 - 270; his miscalculation, 270, 271, 274; on intellectuals' role in revolution, 339

Leontief, Wassily, great tabulation of American industry, 25

Ley, Robert, 595

Liebknecht, Karl, 275

Liebling, A. J., his law, 354, 355

Lincoln, Abraham, congratulated by Marx, 121

Lippmann, Walter, on Roosevelt, 597

Lloyd George, David: on World War I, 233; Keynes on, 345, 346, 366

London: Marx in, 161 - 182; First International born in, 173, 174; Dr. Johnson on, 549

London and County Bank, 293

Lopokova, Lydia, 348

Los Angeles, 374

Louisiana Purchase, 212

Lowell, Abbott Lawrence, 93

Lubin, Isador, 403

Luxembourg, Rosa, 275

Lydia (Asia Minor), invention of coined money, 294, 308

MacArthur, Douglas, 417

McBehan, Harold: and UGE, 465 - 468, 469, 470, 472, 474, 475, 483, 486

McCarthy, Eugene, 589 - 591; and Vietnam war, 601 - 604

McCarthy, Joseph, 412

MacDonald, Ramsay, 241

McGovern, George, 589, 591

machine guns, 250, 251

Macmillan, Harold, on Dulles, 416

Malthus, Rev. Thomas: pessimistic Principle of Population, 44, 56 - 57, 185; on shortage of purchasing power, 48

Manchester, Engels in, 142

Mansfield, Josie, 79, 80

Mao Tse-tung, 411

Marie Antoinette, 24, 25

Marlborough, ninth Duke of, 107

Marshall, Alfred: his economics rendered obsolete by Keynes, 342, 343

Marshall Plan, 391 - 393

Marx, Heinrich, 123

Marx, Jenny (wife), 126, 138, 163, 165, 181

Marx, Jenny (daughter), 181

Marx, Karl, 46, 58, 276, 341, 610; "universal man", 120 - 122; journalism, 120 - 122, 134 - 138, 145 - 147, 161 - 163; birth and early life in Trier, 121 - 126; Jewish ancestry, 123 - 124; atheism and suspected anti-semitism, 124 - 125; at Bonn University, 127; in Berlin, 128 - 133; and Hegel's ideas, 129 - 133; continual harassment by police, 134, 140, 146, 161, 163; in Cologne, 134 - 138; edits

Rheinische Zeitung, 135 - 138; marries Jenny von
Westphalen, 138; in Paris, 138 - 147; edits *German-
French Yearbooks,* 138 - 141; partnership with
Engels, 141 - 142, 147, 162, 172; forms ideas on
Communism, 142 - 153; edits *Vorwärts,* 145 - 147;
in Belgium, 147, 161; composes *Communist
Manifesto,* 147 - 153; and 1848 revolution, 152 - 153,
160; revives *Rheinische Zeitung,* 161; in London,
162 - 167; writes *Das Kapital,* 167 - 171; and
progressive immiseration of workers, 169, 257; helps
to form First International, 173 - 176; and Paris
Commune, 177 - 179; last years, 180 - 182; on
colonialism, 187 - 188, 257; compared with Lenin,
246 - 249; *Address to the Working Classes,* 174; *Civil
War in France,* 179; *Critique of the Gotha
Programme,* 180
Massachusetts, and development of government paper
money, 308, 311
Means, Gardiner C., 471
Mellon, Andrew, 364
Mencken, H. L., on conscience, 116
Menon, Krishna, 225
Merchant City, 545 - 548
Metropolis, 566 - 576; capitalism's failure in, 569 -
570; race prejudice, 567 - 568; social character, 570 -
575
Mexico: revolt against colonialism, 208, 212;
equilibrium of poverty, 517 - 519
Michigan, and bank regulation, 321
Mill, James, 43; and colonialism, 186; *History of
British India,* 186
Mill, John Stuart, 43; and colonialism, 186
Mississippi, 210; migration of rural labor force, 517

Mississippi Company, rise and fall of, 296 - 300
money, 281 - 338; banks, 287 - 308, 315 - 323, 329 -
  332; creation of, 288 - 294, 303; function, 286 - 287;
  gold, 322 - 324, 329; government borrowing and
  spending of, 338, 365 - 367, 371; origins, 284 - 286;
  paper money, 308 - 318; regulation of, 289 - 290,
  299, 303 - 306; value of, Fisher's formula for, 334 -
  336
Moore, G. E., 342
Morgan, J. P., 109, 110, 327, 554
multinational syndrome, 488 - 491
Murphy, Franklin, 604
Murrow, Edward R., 592
Myrdal, Gunnar: and study of national poverty, 508,
  509

Napoleon III, 175, 177, 527
National Recovery Administration (NRA), 369
natural selection: of affluent, 64 - 65, 76; Church and,
  83 - 86
Nehru, Jawaharlal, 96, 429, 608; as a leader, 597 -
  599, 605
Neue Rheinische Zeitung, Marx as editor, 161
Newfoundland Park battlefield, 261, 262
New Harmony (Indiana), 40, 41
New Lanark: Owen's industrial experiment, 38 - 40;
  Institution for the Formation of Character, 39 - 40
New Orleans, 210, 211
Newport (Rhode Island): as monument to conspicuous
  wealth, 95 - 96, 100, 102; "The Breakers," 97
New York: modern rich in, 110, 112; world
  headquarters of UGE, 470
New York Herald, 102

New York Tribune, Marx's journalism for, 120, 163

Niarchos, Stavros, 139

Niebuhr, Reinhold, on Dulles, 418

Nixon, Richard, 430, 466; and détente, 442

Norman, Montagu, 355

North American Defense Command (NORAD), 616

Noske, Gustav, 275

Old Homestead (Ontario), Galbraith family home, 527, 528

Oppenheimer, Robert, 423

O'Reilly, Alexander, 211, 212

Orléans, Philippe, Duc d', and Law's plan for national bank, 294, 295 - 298

Owen, Robert: and New Lanark and New Harmony, 39, 40; influence on Marx, 143

paper money, 308 - 318; revolution financed by, 313

Paris: Marx in, 138 - 147; 1848 Revolution, 152 - 160; Commune of 1871, 177 - 179; UGE operations from, 469, 470

Paterson, William: and Bank of England, 301 - 302

peaceful coexistence, 425, 429

peasants: decisive class in war, 229; not amenable to slaughter, 264 - 265; and power of landlords, 15; role in revolution, 247 - 248, 271

Pentagon, and weapons systems, 422

Peru, Spanish colonization of, 199, 200

Petrograd (now Leningrad), Lenin takes power in, 268, 269

Philadelphia, 549; First International in, 176

Philippines, American colonial experience in, 220

Philips Gloeilampenfabrieken, 478 - 486

Physiocrats, 23, 24, 26

Pitt, William, 49, 303; on Adam Smith, 41, 42

Pizarro, Francisco, 204, 205

Platten, Fritz, 267, 268

playing cards, as currency, 311, 312

Poland: ruled by other East European countries, 231; Lenin in, 230, 242 - 249

Polaris, 444

Political Household, 539 - 544, 550, 573

population explosion, 42 - 47; control of, 506 - 510

Poronin, 244, 249

Port Talbot (Ontario), 524 - 527

Potsdam Conference (1945), 402, 443

poverty, equilibrium of, 37, 499 - 503, 517; breaking of, 502 - 518; city state, 531 - 536; cotton economy, 512 - 518; Mexico, 518 - 521; migration of workers, 521 - 531; Puerto Rico, 518; Punjab, 503 - 505, 510

Powers, Gary, 432, 434

Poznan, 231

Prague, 231

Pravda, Lenin's contributions to, 243

Prescott, W. H., 201, 205

presidential elections, 589 - 595

Principles of Economics (Marshall), 87, 343

Principles of Political Economy (Mill), 186

Principles of Political Economy and Taxation (Ricardo), 185

Progress and Poverty (George), 93

Project Nobska, 443

Proudhon, P. J., 143

Puerto Rico: breaking of equilibrium of poverty, 518

Punjab: British colonization of, 214 - 218; and breaking of equilibrium of poverty, 503 - 505, 510;

birth control, 510
purchasing power, shortage of, Malthus's idea of, 48, 49

Quebec, and paper money, 308, 309, 311, 312, 314
Quesnay, François, 23 - 26; *Tableau Économique,* 25

race prejudice, 565 - 568
Radio Corporation of America, 356
railroads, and affluence from, 75 - 82
Ramage, Rear Admiral L. P., 444
Rand Corporation, 424
reason, men of, 20 - 22
Rembrandt, 292
revolution: financing by paper money, 313 - 314;
    Lenin's view of, 247 - 249, 259; Marx's view of, 258;
    peasants' role in, 247 - 248; three conditions for,
    156 - 157
Rheinische Zeitung, Marx as editor of, 134 - 138
Rhodes, Knights Hospitallers in, 197
Ricardo, David, 43, 118, 303; his labor theory of value,
    45 - 48, 56, 168; on landlords' revenue, 47 - 48; and
    colonialism, 185   186
right to work, as motive of 1848 Revolution, 154, 155
Rist, Charles, 355
Riviera, its service to the rich, 105 - 106, 108
Robbins, Lionel, 364
Rockefeller, John D., 61, 73
Rockefeller, Nelson A.: on dangers of compassion, 74,
    75
Roll, Sir Eric, on motivating influence on capitalist
    change, 144
Roosevelt, Franklin D., 608; puzzled by Keynes, 367,
    368; as a leader, 596, 599

Rosenberg, Alfred, 9
Rostow, Walt W., 600
Ruge, Arnold, 140, 141
Runnymede, 15
Rusk, Dean, 440
Russia (*see also* Soviet Union): Revolution, 157, 247 -
  248, 265 - 270, 313; pre-1914 Empire, 230; alliances,
  232 - 233; and World War I, 241, 265; Lenin takes
  power, 268

Saint-Simon, Duc de, 143, 154, 301, 309
Samuelson, Paul A., 380, 452, 453
Say, Jean Baptiste, 48
Schacht, Hjalmar, 355, 367
Schumpeter, Joseph A., 120, 364, 374, 539
Schurz, Carl, 72
Scopes, John T., 84
Scotland, and Clearances, 33 - 37, 512, 561
Seaboard Airline, 356
Second Bank of the United States, 318, 319
Second International, 176
self-interest, and wealth of nations, 28, 41
Seville, Archivo General de Indias in, 203
Shaplen, Robert, 86
Shaw, George Bernard, 370
Shenandoah Corporation, 358, 359, 416
Simpson, Joe (Skidoo murderer), 613
Singapore: multinational presence in, 488, 489; as
  prosperous city-state, 531 - 536
Six, Jan (Rembrandt), 292
Skidoo 23 (California), 612 - 614
Small, Howard J: and UGE, 475, 476, 479, 483, 486;
  on danger of socialism, 495 - 498

Smith, Adam, 16 - 34, 70, 118, 533, 610; as first
economist, 16 - 20, 41 - 42; academic career, 18 - 19;
Grand Tour, 20 - 27; impressed by France and
Physiocrats, 20 - 26; as man of reason, 22, 59;
rejects Quesnay's *Tableau,* 25; on division of labor,
28 - 30; on combinations and corporations, 31 - 33,
44, 578; his economic model, 42; optimism
contrasted with Ricardo and Malthus, 47 - 48; and
colonialism, 184 - 185, 200; *Wealth of Nations,* 20,
27 - 33, 49
Social Darwinism, 65 - 73
Social Democrats: and World War I, 239 - 241, 247;
Zimmerwald conference (1915), 255
Somme, Battle of (1916), 260, 261
South Sea Bubble, 303, 307
Soviet Union (*see also* Russia): colonialism, 223;
agriculture, 272, 363; automobile industry, 273;
collectivization, 363; arms competition with
America, 443 - 448; consolidation in Eastern Europe,
405, 411; and Berlin blockade, 409 - 412; and Korea,
411; Cold War, 412, 418 - 420, 427 - 442; and Cuba,
433; and Vietnam, 441; and deténte, 442
Spain, and colonial achievement, 198 - 210
Spanish-American War, 220
Spencer, Herbert, 118 - 119; as the great Social
Darwinist, 66 - 74; originator of "survival of
fittest," 66; and ascent of privileged classes, 67 - 68;
allows charity, 69; American tour, 71 - 74; Beecher
and, 73, 84 - 86
Stalin, Joseph, 363, 405, 428, 429; policies reversed by
Khrushchev, 429, 430; and atomic bomb, 443
Steffens, Lincoln, 557
Stevenson, Adlai, 433, 589; on Riviera, 105; on Korea,

657

411; and Cuban missile crisis, 437

stock market speculation (1927 - 29), 356 - 362

Stokes, Edward, 80

Strathnaver, Highland Clearances, 35

Streicher, Julius, 11, 595

Strong, Benjamin, 331

Suez crisis (1956), 417

Sumner, William Graham, 89, 118; as Social Darwinist, 70, 71, 74

supermarkets, 282, 283

Sutherland, Highland Clearances, 35 - 37, 512

Sweezy, Paul M., 121

Switzerland: Lenin in, 249, 252 - 259, 265 - 267; as revolutionary capital of world, 252; race prejudice, 565; democratic example, 580 - 586

Tableau Économique (Quesnay), 25

Talbot, Colonel Thomas, and settlement of Port Talbot, 524 - 527

Taylor, A. J. P., 233

Taylor, Maxwell, 600

Tell, William, 581

Teller, Edward, 444

Templars, 196

Tennessee Coal and Iron Company, 554

territorial imperative, 233 - 236

Teutonic Knights, 196

Texas, the modern rich in, 113

textile revolution, 12, 512, 513

textile town, New Lanark as model, 38 - 40

Theory of Business Enterprise, The (Veblen), 94

Theory of the Leisure Class, The (Veblen), 93 - 95

Theirs, Adolphe, 178; Marx on, 173

Third World: Marx's standing in, 188; Canada and
    United States as first countries of, 531
Tilton, Elizabeth, 86
Times, The, attack on Keynes, 346
Togliattigrad, automobile industry, 273
Trevelyan, Charles Edward, 53, 54
Trier: Marx's early life in, 122 - 127
Trotsky, Leon, 245
Truman, Harry S., 443
Turgot, Anne Robert Jacques, 26, 27
Turin, automobile industry, 273
Tweed, Boss, 79

underemployment equilibrium, 371
unemployment, 352, 353, 392; Hitler's cure for, 366 -
    367, 381; Keynes's remedy for, 366 - 367, 371, 380 -
    382, 388
Unified Global Enterprises (UGE): as illustration of
    corporate development, 459 - 477; founding of, 459 -
    465; changes of name, 462 - 466; present-day,
    465 - 469; Era of McBehan, 465 - 468, 472, 483, 486;
    overseas operations, 469 - 470; control of, 470 - 473;
    Washington office, 473 - 474; technostructure, 475 -
    477; reason for unease, 485 - 487; and multinational
    syndrome, 488 - 491
United States of America: emigration to, 55 - 58, 186,
    562 - 563; and Social Darwinism, 70 - 74; railroad
    struggle, 75 - 79; high capitalism in, 75 - 117;
    reconciliation of natural selection with Christian
    faith, 83 - 86; Conspicuous Leisure and Conspicuous
    Consumption, 95 - 99; publicity, 101 - 102;
    marriages with European aristocracy, 106 - 108; the
    modern rich, 110 - 117; painful colonial experience,

218 - 222; aid to India, 225; pre-1914 industrial
proletariat, 228; and World War I, 263; ruling
coalition of capitalists and workers, 276; and
invention of paper money, 308 - 309, 313 - 314;
financing of Revolution, 313; banks and the central
banks, 315 - 322, 326 - 329; struggle between
political and banking power, 318 - 322, 329; and
gold, 324, 354 - 355; stock market speculation, 330,
356 - 362; Great Depression, 328 - 332, 362 - 365,
368 - 369, 596; and Keynesian Revolution, 374 - 381,
388 - 395; recovery and further recession, 377 - 380;
price control, 384 - 387; aid to Europe, 393;
arms race with Soviet Union, 396 - 399, 443 - 447;
close relationship between industry and armed
services, 399, 407, 422 - 423, 431, 445 - 448; Berlin
airlift, 409; Cold War, 412 - 415, 424, 431 - 442; and
Korea, 411; and Cuba, 432 - 435; and Vietnam, 438 -
442, 600 - 604; and big corporations, 459 - 477, 488 -
498; cotton economy and equilibrium of poverty,
512 - 518; as first country of Third World, 531;
agricultural labor force, 537; race prejudice 565; and
leadership instinct, 586 - 587, 595 - 597; presidential
elections, 589 - 594, 602 - 603
United States Steel Corporation, 554
Urban II, Pope, and real motive of Crusades, 193

Valladolid, 205
Vanderbilt, Consuelo, 107
Vanderbilt, Cornelius, 114 - 115; and Erie Railroad
  struggle, 76 - 80; policy of robbing the public, 77,
  82; and Conspicuous Consumption, 97, 106
Vanderbilt, William K., 106
Vanderbilt University (Nashville), 97

Veblen, Thorstein, 87 - 95, 118, 333; his view of the American rich, 87, 89 - 90, 95, 97 - 98; eccentric life, 91 - 93; on distinction between makers and moneymakers, 94; Conspicuous Leisure and Conspicuous Consumption, 93 - 95, 99, 108; *Theory of Business Enterprise,* 94; *Theory of the Leisure Class,* 93 - 95

Venice, 545, 546

Verdun, 261

Versailles: "Le Hameau," 24

Versailles Treaty, signing of, 346

Vietnam war, 438 - 442; American intervention, 221 - 222, 278, 600 - 602; relationship between leadership and commitment, 600 - 604

Voltaire: as man of reason, 21, 22

Vorwärts, Marx's work for, 145 - 147

wages: cuts in, 352, 353, 364; law of, 168, 365

Walker, James J., 369

Wall Street Crash, 359 - 362

Warsaw, 231

Washington, D.C.: and Cold War, 421 - 424; and Keynesian Revolution, 376 - 387; UGE in, 473, 474

Washington, George, 317

Wealth of Nations, An Inquiry into the Nature and Causes of the (Smith), 20, 27 - 33, 49

Western Europe: pre-1914 ruling class and capitalists, 228; industrial proletariat, 228; pre-1914 imperialism, 232; and World War I, 238 - 241, 260 - 265, 275; quiet revolution, 275 - 276; coalition of capitalists and workers, 276; failure of capitalism in health and housing, 569 - 570

Westphalen, Baron Ludwig von, 126

White, Harry D., 389
Whitney, Richard, 361
William of Orange, 301
Wilson, Woodrow: Keynes on, 345
Wood, Charles, 53
workers: coalition with capitalists after World War I, 276; and law of wages, 45; migration to industrialized countries, 521 - 523, 561 - 568; overthrow of capitalism, 130, 170 - 171, 257 - 258; and power of landlords, 15, 46 - 47; pre-1914 political force, 229; support for World War I, 238 - 241, 247 - 249, 274 - 275
World War I: collapse of political and social systems in, 227 - 229, 276 - 280, 285; causes of, 233 - 239; workers' reaction, 238 - 241, 247 - 249, 274 - 275; stupidity and slaughter, 250 - 251, 259 - 265; heroism a matter of rank not courage, 263 - 264; end, 275; Peace Treaty, 344 - 346
World War II: as watershed of change, 226; benefit to American business, 406 - 408

Young, Andrew, 604

Zimmerwald, socialists' conference (1915), 255
Zurich, Lenin in, 265, 266